What Ever Happened to the Baptism in the Holy Spirit?

Loren VanGalder

Spiritual Father Publications

ISBN: 978-1-7336556-8-2

Contents

Introduction

What ever happened to the baptism in the Holy Spirit?

That's a strange question, isn't it? God's Word does not change. Jesus promised to baptize us in the Spirit, and the church in Acts displayed the dynamic fulfillment of that promise. However, it did not stop there: The church fathers Irenaeus and Tertullian spoke favorably of the baptism, charismatic gifts were common in the Montanist movement of the late second century, and Orthodox monasteries in the Middle Ages reported speaking in tongues, as did French Huguenots and Jansenists.

And yet, even though there have been experiences of the Spirit and speaking in tongues throughout church history, centuries passed when the baptism of the Spirit was rarely mentioned and the accompanying gifts unused. That all changed with the Pentecostal and Charismatic renewals of the twentieth century, and today the majority of the world's Christians are in churches that believe in the baptism and spiritual gifts. But a strange thing is happening: Even in those churches, many are unsure if they have received the baptism, and it is rarely preached about.

Australian David Perry, in his excellent thesis Pentecostal Spirit baptism: An analysis of meaning and function, writes:

> There has been a recent trend, evident in both Pentecostal scholarship and Pentecostal praxis, towards the displacement of Spirit baptism as the central Pentecostal distinctive and a lessening of the emphasis given to this experience. With Pentecostal identity at a crossroads,

1

there is a very real possibility that Spirit baptism will be marginalized to the point that it becomes practically insignificant.

This striking statement comes from the former field director of Assemblies of God missions in Mexico, who has traveled and ministered extensively in Latin America for twenty-five years:

In a local church setting, I do not think I have ever heard anyone preach about the Baptism of the Spirit. That includes Costa Rica, Peru, Mexico, and anywhere else that I have been involved in a TEE (Theological Education by Extension) seminar. I cannot recall a single instance when a pastor invited people to receive the Baptism of the Spirit.

What is the baptism?

Author, professor, and theologian Frank D. Macchia captured the essence of Spirit baptism in his book Baptized in the Spirit:

God's people are carried by Spirit baptism on the winds of God's holy breath to bear witness to Christ. They come to know that divine freedom as their own when they lay down their limited imaginations and are overtaken by God's missionary passion for the world. The self-giving God of Spirit baptism produces a self-giving people in mission. The God who seeks to save the lost produces a people who do the same. To love God is to be shaped by that love so as to share its affections and passions. Spirit baptism is not mere empowerment for mission in Pentecostal interpretation, even though it has that focus. If it were, there would be no way of accounting for the equally important Pentecostal stress on the greater intimacy with God and fervency in eschatological expectation that characterize Pentecostal testimonies of Spirit baptism. Spirit baptism is akin to a prophetic call that draws believers closer to His heart in deeper love and empathy, enabling them to catch a glimpse of the divine love for the world. It is this love that is at the substance of the power for mission. It is in the realm of the Spirit that I participate in the *koinonia* of divine love with others...It is in the realm of the Spirit that I join my heart with the one who so loves the world and sent the divine Son to seek and to save the lost. It is on the winds of the Spirit that we are consecrated and called for a holy task and empowered to go forth as a vessel for the salvation of others, burning with the love of God for them. It is in the Spirit and the love of Christ that we confront injustice with a passion for the liberty and dignity of those who are oppressed, as well as the transformation of those who benefit intentionally or blindly from that oppression.

This is the ultimate in God's plan for his adopted sons and daughters. It won't get any better than this until heaven! So why aren't we talking about it more? Why do people somehow feel ashamed or afraid to mention the baptism or minister it? Is it Satan's way of robbing the church of its power? Or has the church once again "lost its first love" amid its success and comfort? The baptism in the Spirit needs to regain the emphasis it deserves; not just talking about it, but daily experiencing the Spirit as Macchia describes it. At this point in history, we need it more than ever.

Part One

Touched by the Spirit

Chapter 1

The Historical Context

The modern Pentecostal movement is rooted in the Second Great Awakening and Holiness revivals of the second half of the 19th century. The first modern recorded experiences of the baptism and speaking in tongues were at a Bible college in Topeka, Kansas. A student from the college began ministering at the Azusa Street Mission in Los Angeles in 1906, and the revival began. Three services were held every day for over three years. Participants tended to be from the margins of society, and most Christians viewed it as extreme or even dangerous, calling them "holy rollers," "holy jumpers," or even "snake handlers" (for the small segment that literally practiced Mark 16:18).

Pentecostals were full of evangelistic and missionary zeal, and some of the first missionaries took the message of Pentecost to Latin America. Traditional evangelical missions had labored with limited success for years, but Pentecostalism has flourished and become the predominant Christian movement in most of the developing world. Some estimates number Pentecostal/charismatic Christians at 500 million.

The healing revivalists of the 1950s (including Oral Roberts, William Branham, T.L. Osborn, and Kathryn Kuhlman) and groups like Demos Shakarian's Full Gospel Business Men's Fellowship paved the way for a broader movement. My mother, who was not Pentecostal, loved watching Oral Roberts on TV. On Easter Sunday, 1960, Dennis Bennett, rector of an Episcopal church in Van Nuys, California (less than twenty miles from Azusa Street), shared that he had received the baptism of the Holy Spirit. The charismatic renewal (from the Greek word *"charism"*, meaning "gift of grace") in mainline protestant and Catholic churches had begun. *Time*, *Newsweek*, and national television covered "Pentecostalism entering the mainline," although there was little interaction with the traditional Pentecostals, at least initially. Not everyone was happy with Bennett's announcement; he resigned from the church and was reassigned to a church in Seattle, which became a leader in the charismatic movement. He also wrote a popular book, "Nine O'Clock in the Morning."

One of the most common (and controversial) experiences of those receiving the baptism was speaking in other tongues. Some traditional Pentecostal bodies, such as the Assemblies of God, include speaking in tongues as the essential sign of the baptism in their statement of faith. John and Elizabeth Sherrill introduced it to a broad audience with their book They Speak With Other Tongues, still one of the best accounts of the early charismatic movement. The popular singer Pat Boone wrote about his experience in his autobiography A New Song. The Jesus Movement of the early 1970s overlapped significantly with the charismatic renewal; perhaps the majority of the hippies and young people who came to Christ also received the baptism in the Spirit.

The common experience of the baptism erased differences between Catholics and Protestants, hippies and businessmen, young and old, and rich and poor. Growing numbers who had received the baptism felt uncomfortable in their mainline or Catholic churches, and increasingly migrated to independent churches. In the process, they unfortunately lost the theological moorings and oversight of the traditional churches, resulting in untrained clergy and theological aberrations. Gradually, as often happens in revivals, the baptism in the Spirit became more institutionalized. The Assemblies of God has become a mainstream, respected denomination and one of the fastest-growing groups in the nation and the world. The focus on the baptism and tongues gradually faded to the point that today, Assemblies leaders express concern about the decline in the number of those experiencing the baptism with speaking in tongues.

Beginning in the 1980s, there was a "Third Wave" or "neo-charismatic" movement (the Pentecostal revival being the first and the charismatic movement the second). Chuck Smith (Calvary Chapel), John Wimber (Vineyard), and missiologist C. Peter Wagner were significant early leaders. The emphasis is on signs and wonders, and even though there is evident belief in the Spirit's power, they do not view a second experience called the Baptism of the Holy Spirit as necessary. Partly through their influence, there has been increasing acceptance of some spiritual gifts and "charismatic" worship in the broader evangelical movement, and a definite de-emphasis of the baptism of the Holy Spirit.

What has happened to these experiences?

Some things that were common during the height of the charismatic renewal are rare today, such as:

Spirit-led, spontaneous worship. In many places, it was common to have a worship leader with a guitar or keyboard who would wait on the Lord and sense the Spirit's leading for what to sing. There was a spontaneity and freshness in the worship, and simplicity in the songs and music. Professional-sounding bands have largely replaced that with carefully planned sets of today's most popular worship songs. With the often-deafening noise, flashing lights, and smoke, it can be challenging to know if it is really about worshipping Jesus or enjoying a great band with emotional music. It is not uncommon to see the majority of the congregation not even singing. On various occasions, I have heard people refer to the worship service as a "show." That does not mean that authentic worship does not take place in those services; God can indeed be glorified, and there are many sincere worship leaders and musicians and beautiful worship songs.

Small groups frequently followed Paul's instructions in 1 Corinthians 14:26: *When you come together, each of you has a hymn, or a word of instruction, a revelation, a tongue or an interpretation. Everything must be done so that the church may be built up.* The Holy Spirit truly led, as one person would share a Scripture, another would start a song, someone would pray, and another would bring a prophetic word.

Singing in the Spirit. Paul discusses this in 1 Corinthians 14:15: the Spirit takes over the music with amazing harmonies as musicians play and the congregation sings "a new song," whether in tongues or in English. Some have suggested that Gregorian chants evolved from this practice. There seems to be little room for it in today's scripted services, and no guidance from worship leaders or pastors to help the congregation enter in. Its absence may be due to the small number who are baptized in the Spirit, or not allowing the Spirit freedom to move.

Prophetic words. In many services, there would be an evident, Spirit-led pause after the worship, when the atmosphere was heavy with his presence. During that time, someone might bring forth a message in tongues, followed by an interpretation. If there seemed to be a delay in that interpretation, a pastor might say, "Pray for the interpretation," and we would wait for it. Or a message might be given in English. There were people in the church recognized as having a gift of discernment; if there were questions about the message truly being of the Spirit, they would gently suggest that it might not be a prophetic word. There were abuses associated with these words, and a degree of discernment and authority is necessary in the leadership to allow them to flow correctly. Some churches require a word to be approved by the leadership before being given. The reality in many "mega churches" is that there simply is not time or the ability to accommodate these words. Instead of waiting for the Spirit to speak, many churches move right into the offering, or a video of announcements, or welcome to the church. Where prophecy is recognized, it is often predictive or corrective, instead of what Paul presents in 1 Corinthians 14:3: *The one who prophesies speaks to people for their strengthening, encouraging and comfort.*

Chapter 2

My Experience

I grew up in a mainline, somewhat liberal, Congregational Church (later part of the United Church of Christ). My family had daily devotions and a strong faith, but I don't remember hearing anything about the Holy Spirit at home. Most references at church were to the "Holy Ghost," reflecting the King James Version translation of the word for Spirit. We sang about him weekly in the Doxology and the Gloria Patri, and occasionally in hymns; otherwise, he was rarely mentioned. For many years, I pictured him as a ghost, somewhat like Casper the Friendly Ghost.

I left home to attend college, eager to experience the world, but for the first time, I encountered vibrant Christians my age. I struggled to admit that I was a sinner in need of a Savior, but in February of my freshman year, I accepted Christ into my life. My older sister, who received Christ in college, was studying for her master's at a nearby seminary. She had been very involved with Inter-Varsity Christian Fellowship and provided a steady supply of IVP books. I began a daily devotional time and studied the Scriptures, giving me a strong foundation for my new life.

A second blessing?

Some friends from the campus fellowship invited me to attend a house church, where I was exposed to raised hands and charismatic worship for the first time. They also talked about spiritual gifts, which I had never heard of, and somebody gave me a book by Merlin Carothers called <u>Prison</u> <u>to</u> <u>Praise</u>, in which he described his baptism in the Spirit (see Appendix 2). That was new to me and left me a little confused. I thought I had taken care of everything when I accepted Christ, but now I learned that apparently there was a second step involved.

That summer, at home, I came across a booklet by Bill Bright of Campus Crusade for Christ called <u>Have</u> <u>You</u> <u>Made</u> <u>the</u> <u>Wonderful</u> <u>Discovery</u> <u>of</u> <u>the</u> <u>Spirit-filled</u> <u>Life?</u> Campus Crusade was famous for its evangelistic booklet <u>Have</u> <u>You</u> <u>Heard</u> <u>of</u> <u>the</u> <u>Four</u> <u>Spiritual</u> <u>Laws?</u> The follow-up booklet presents the Spirit-filled life as a deeper life that Christ intends for us. I have included it in Appendix 1 (thanks to Campus Crusade, now called CRU) and encourage you to read it. I prayed the prayer and felt I was one step closer to experiencing the fullness of the Spirit. Yet it avoided the term "baptism in the Spirit" or any mention of speaking in tongues, which seemed to be a significant part of my friends' experience. I still felt that there was something more.

The concept of a second blessing or deeper spiritual experience has been expressed in various ways since the foundation of the church, including monasticism, pietism, and fringe groups such as the Quakers. There was resistance in many evangelical circles to the baptism as a second experience; the respected English pastor John Stott wrote a book called <u>Baptism</u> <u>and</u> <u>Fullness</u>, which argued that what many called the baptism was simply an experience of the fullness of the Spirit. The many different approaches left me confused, yet if there was something more, I was determined to experience it.

I receive the baptism

That fall, back at college, I became more deeply involved in the campus fellowship and the house church. Someone gave me another book by Merlin Carothers called Power in Praise. One day, while reading it alone in a college lounge, I felt moved to start praising God. Without thinking about it or asking for it, I suddenly found myself praising God in tongues. It flowed like a river from deep within me for over an hour. When I shared with others what had happened, they confirmed that I had experienced the baptism. My spiritual life was transformed; I couldn't get enough of God, of prayer and praise, and of fellowship with other believers. The Bible came alive. Speaking to others about Christ, which had been difficult for me, came naturally, and God provided many opportunities to witness. A journal entry from a few days later gives an idea of what I was experiencing:

> While in prayer in the Browsing Room tonight I came into the presence of God as never before. I felt like getting down on the floor, His greatness was so mighty. The light was near blinding. Jesus Christ was right beside me, real as life. I was afraid to lift my head; I thought angels would be in the room. Praise the Lord! Jesus is my Lord and Savior!

A second baptism in Mexico

A year and a half later, I was now leading the campus fellowship and preparing to spend the summer as a missionary in Mexico. I had left the house church and was attending a Baptist church, and was heavily involved with Inter-Varsity, which took a neutral stance on the baptism. When I arrived in Mexico, I found many in the student movement who loved Jesus, but had never experienced the baptism. I did fellowship with some who had, and joined them at Catholic charismatic praise services. I was hungry for God and the vitality I had previously known, and I began spending extended time in prayer, praise, and the Scriptures in the library of the Bible Institute where I was living. My journal entry from June 30, 1976, explains what happened next:

> Hallelujah! I feel like I got a whole new beginning today. Just didn't feel like doing anything in the morning – finally started reading a book called The Man God Uses. Excellent book, and what really hit me was what it said about prayer and Quiet Time. What I've known all along. Really felt like I should pray after I had read it, but sat around for a couple hours. Finally went up to a music classroom. I felt I had to break through something, and as I sat there praising God I started speaking in tongues – the first time in a year and a half. It was great! I felt like there was so much my spirit wanted to get out and finally it had a chance. Prayed for over half an hour in tongues – felt like I knew what I was praying for. Afterward spent almost an hour in joyful song to the Lord. And all night I've noticed a real difference. Even the dog was super friendly, I really enjoyed the sunset, had a good talk with my roommate, then went to the Stewart's [the missionaries I was working with] and had letters waiting for me. Later I ran into this crippled guy and found out he's really lonely and having a rough time. He was happy to talk with me.

It was a second baptism in the Spirit, and there was an immediate transformation in the effectiveness of my ministry.

A third baptism?

After college, I joined the staff of Inter-Varsity in New York City and got involved in an Assemblies of God church. Many of the students on campus came from traditional Pentecostal churches, and I found myself among people very familiar with the baptism. I thought everything was fine until an evangelist from a very charismatic Jewish messianic ministry called B'Nai Yeshua came to City College, where I was on staff. After he shared in the fellowship meeting, we went for lunch, and he asked me if I was baptized in the Spirit and spoke in tongues. I was a little annoyed that he would even ask me, and quickly responded "of course," as if to say, "if there is anything to experience as a Christian, I have it." It was a common expression in many city churches to say I'm "saved, sanctified, and filled with the Holy Ghost," and I certainly felt like I was. I was further annoyed when he brushed away my assurances and said God was telling him to pray for me to be baptized in the Spirit. My journal entry from March 30, 1978, records what happened:

> A truly significant day. This Jewish guy Fred came in from Stonybrook to see the city schools. I felt a real lack of direction for what he should do. I don't think it was that good a time for him. But we started talking, and it drifted around to the topic of the Holy Spirit. As he started describing what the Holy Spirit could do, and getting to the depth of my own problems with an insight I knew was only from God, I became both uneasy and filled with anticipation. It was really harmful to my pride, as I had always been able to confidently say I'd been baptized in the Spirit and spoke in tongues (I wonder how much I liked being able to <u>say</u> that?). Anyway, he asked to pray for the baptism for me. I rejected the idea of praying for it in the cafeteria, and we went outside. He laid hands on me, and prayed – part in tongues – for me. I obediently prayed in tongues but didn't really feel anything. He also prayed for friends (a couple) for me – he sensed this to be a real need. He indicated that he didn't think the case was that my life was falling apart, but just that God wanted so much more.

He left, and I shared it with Carlos [a student leader in the fellowship], who was really excited. Then I came home and read <u>Risky</u> <u>Living</u> – very helpful. Went out in the park for a delightful hour of prayer and sensing a lot of sin. Later in the evening I really got into a frenzied time of prayer. Went into a very strange tongue and really focused on Jesus Christ. Felt so clean…so much at peace. Feel this is the beginning of something new and important – and much needed. I am so thankful for Fred, and the very obvious way God brought him into my life.

I became convicted of all kinds of sin in my life; not things we usually think of as sin, but things like arrogance and a cooling of my first love. I got down on my face and started pouring out my broken heart in confession and repentance, and had what was one of the clearest "visions" I have ever had in my life, of Jesus on the cross. His love washed over me, and the tongues, which had been largely absent from my life for months, flowed once again. Immediately, my ministry changed, similar to what I had experienced twice before. People asked me about the baptism in the Spirit. I spoke with new authority and boldness in evangelism and teaching. My devotional life came alive. The anointing continued until I went to summer camps, where the manifestation of spiritual gifts and freedom for the Spirit was discouraged. I saw opportunities to minister, but felt constrained, and gradually the Spirit was grieved and started to withdraw.

I wish I could say that my life in the Spirit has seen steady growth in the many years since then, but, like many Christians, I have faced struggles along the way. I have found that daily Quiet Time is essential to staying close to the Lord, as well as participating in a healthy church. I can pretty much track my spiritual health to my praying in tongues: when tongues are flowing, I am much more in the Spirit; when several days pass without praying in tongues, I know my heart has gotten a little cold. My growing concern about the silence of the church regarding the baptism led me to talk with many others, who I found had similar concerns. The next chapter includes some of their testimonies.

Chapter 3

Testimonies

The Night the Power Fell at Leavenworth Penitentiary

The year was 1990. I was facing life in prison without the possibility of parole. I was scheduled for sentencing the following morning. I was a new Christian. Just before bed, I felt convicted to pray before going to sleep. I asked my co-defendant, Sal, who had been born again for about six months, and our other roommate, Big George, to pray with me. They looked at me with pity and said, "Sure." I felt the need to get out of bed and kneel on the cold cement floor as an act of humility before God. Sal and George remained on their beds a short distance from me in that 8' X 16' cell. As we began to pray, the atmosphere was no different from normal. It was a cold-floored prison cell. I began to pray aloud, asking for the Lord's mercy, wisdom, and favor to go before me at sentencing the following day. After praying for just a few minutes, God's presence began to enter the room. The atmosphere was totally transformed. My prayer began to take on a completely new dimension. Clarity and authority were suddenly in my voice. Faith filled my soul. Something special was happening. Then an utterance in tongues bubbled forth forcefully from deep within my belly. I had never experienced such a flow. Prior to this, I had experienced the Spirit moving my mouth as I prayed, but this was something much deeper. It was power such as I'd never experienced before. At first, it startled me, but I had a peace that passed all understanding. I yielded to the Spirit. I would pray in English, and then an utterance in tongues, beyond my understanding, would flow forth. Then back to English, my native tongue, with my understanding, then in tongues again. Sal began to experience the complimentary gift, the interpretation of tongues. Whatever flowed out of me in this unknown language, Sal was supernaturally hearing back in his mind clearly in English. Sal began to speak out the interpretation as I would pause for him to speak. It was amazingly natural, although clearly supernatural. We were flowing in the Spirit together with tongues and interpretation of tongues, just as the Bible said was possible. I had been saved for only a month when this occurred. It was a wonderful and invigorating time in God's presence. The majority of prayers we were led to pray that night were answered within the next 72 hours in miraculous ways. God had shown up in a dirty prison cell in Leavenworth Penitentiary, confirming his presence and power to a couple of repentant criminals. From that day forward, I have prayed in tongues every day, and on many occasions have experienced interpretation of tongues with prayers being specifically answered identical to the words of the interpretation given.

An MK (Missionary Kid)

I experienced the baptism of the Holy Spirit at a Christian fellowship group in Holland, Michigan, while I was a freshman at Hope College (1972 – 1973). I was interested in it because my own parents, who were Presbyterian missionaries serving in Seoul, Korea, wrote to me in their letters about receiving it. I felt that if it was good enough for my parents who I loved and admired, then it was good enough for me. I could trust it; it wasn't just a fad of some sort. I had been exposed to it years earlier when I was a child attending a church service around the DMZ in Korea. My father was speaking at this military service and afterwards some of the soldiers met together, praying in tongues. I found it fascinating. My parents (who weren't baptized in the Spirit yet) told me that some of these men were Pentecostal and worshiped this way.

I received the Holy Spirit in the typical way most did back then, with the laying on of hands. I was instructed to open my mouth and allow sounds to come out. Eventually, other students were praying for me, and then I started praying in sounds that I did not understand. I was instructed to "keep it up" or practice it daily. I did continue to pray in the spirit the rest of the year. It is still part of my prayer life, although I will confess that at times I use it more when I am under "stress" and need the stilling presence of the Holy Spirit or need direction. I can pray silently in the Spirit, so if I am around other Christians who do not welcome this, I can still communicate with the Father and not offend anyone. Currently my husband and I are members of a Lutheran church which does not embrace this aspect of the Holy Spirit. The church does speak about the Holy Spirit and about the day of Pentecost and certainly upholds the Holy Spirit's work in people's lives, but there is no "laying on of hands" and speaking in tongues. When my husband and I pray together in our own prayer time or concerning an issue we are questioning in our lives, we do pray in the spirit.

If someone asked me to help them receive the baptism, I would probably pray with them and follow the example done for me. I would read the scriptures about being filled with the Holy Spirit. I haven't had anyone ask for this in a long time, probably due to the fact that I don't belong to a fellowship that recognizes this infilling.

A pastor in the Chicago area

My journey started in the winter of 1974, when we were invited to a short Bible Study (6 weeks) on faith and the book of Acts.

The discussion and study was interesting, but made no lasting impression on me. It did influence Penny, as she expressed an interest in receiving the Baptism of the Holy Spirit. Rick gave her a book about how to receive the Holy Spirit Baptism and within a short time, while at home, she received this experience with the evidence of speaking in a new language. However, she did not share this experience with me for months. At the conclusion of the study, Rick asked if I wanted him to pray with me and I said no.

In October, we were made aware of a Charismatic retreat being held in Franklin Park at a Methodist church. Here was an opportunity. Together with a young lady named Julie, who had joined the Methodist church we were attending, we journeyed to Franklin Park for the one day event. Julie, originally from Iowa, had received the Baptism in the Holy Spirit along with most of the youth from her church. She was a student at a nursing school in Evanston. It was a warm evening when Penny and Julie began praying with me to receive the Baptism in the Holy Spirit. This was the first time I had ever heard Penny pray in her new language. I did not receive anything from God and my shirt was soaked with sweat.

At times I felt like Simon (Acts 8:9–24) had the right idea, that it would be easier to buy the gift. As I think back on my situation, it was really a matter of pride. I had an abundance of pride. I felt there was nothing I could not do myself in this world. In November of 1975, Rick wrote that he was attending a home church meeting in Lake Villa on a Monday night in early December. Penny and I agreed to attend. The worship lasted one hour and was really interesting. Penny raised her hands and sang in her new language. At the close of the meeting, Rick once again asked if I was interested in having him pray with me to receive the Baptism in the Holy Spirit. As before, I said no. However, I did promise that I would pray by myself the following night at home.

I took my Bible and a book to the basement and sat at a card table in the bedroom. I had never spent any time with God alone, so I was somewhat afraid, having no idea what was going to happen. I read the Book of Acts again and skimmed a book written by Hobart Freeman on how to receive the Baptism in the Holy Spirit. One of the steps he suggested was praying for forgiveness. I thought about that for a while and realized that at no time in my life had I ever received Jesus as my Lord and Savior. I had obviously fooled everyone, including myself, but God knew. I then starting praying, telling God that tonight was my night to finally ask for forgiveness of sins, regardless of what I had prayed for in the past. I was drawing a line on my past life of sin. My heart was broken. I yielded everything I was to Him as my Lord and Savior. It may not have been a model prayer, but God knew my heart. I was His man.

That prayer, which was probably the first prayer I had ever spoken aloud to God in my life, brought some relief and optimism. It certainly gave me some faith. My focus then turned to the Baptism in the Holy Spirit, with the evidence of speaking in a new language. I had heard too many testimonies to doubt that it was from God, nor was anyone denied who wanted this experience. I also knew that everyone had a different experience in receiving this Baptism. The first thing I did was to ask God for the Baptism in the Holy Spirit, and the tongues which provided the evidence, in the name of Jesus. As before on other occasions, nothing happened. Speaking means moving the vocal cords. I could do that and see what happened. I decided to begin singing, and when I did, I started singing words I did not know. It was only a few words, and some repeated, but I was ecstatic. I continued on, but then went quiet for a short time, just thanking God for what He had just blessed me with.

I then started speaking again aloud, but in English this time. I will never forget the words. "I will never leave you, nor forsake you, not now, nor till the end of time." I knew immediately that this was a message from God to me. Words of assurance and comfort that I could hold in my heart forever, a personal prophecy. Someone might say, "But this is similar to Hebrews 13:5." That is true, but I had no idea that some of those words were in the Bible, for I did not spend time reading the Bible, except the book of Acts.

Following that night, the floodgates of Heaven opened. I continued to pray in the Holy Spirit (my language expanded), started listening to teaching tapes (cassettes at the time), and began reading the Bible. I had promised my parents that Penny and I would come to their home in Topeka, Kansas for Christmas. As typically happens, I could not wait to share everything that God had done in my life. When Penny and I shared our testimonies, my mother asked if I was sure that tongues were not from the devil. I was shocked, for I assumed she would embrace what we were experiencing. I later realized that that this was not an unusual response. Several years later I learned that Charles Parham, a Methodist, who started Bethel Bible School in Topeka Kansas, prayed for and received with his students the Baptism in the Holy Spirit in January of 1901. This experience sparked the beginning of the Pentecostal movement.

Louis Osterberg

Little by little I felt the power fall. To make a long story short, I was soon speaking in other tongues, and the blessed experience gained then I cannot tell in words, for they would fail to express the divine meaning which it has to my soul. I spoke in tongues for nearly three hours and glorified God in them. During this time, God revealed much to me which I will not at this time relate. I did not think it possible for a human being to be so filled with God's glory. I now begin to comprehend with all saints what is the breadth and length, and depth, and height, and to know the love of Christ which passeth knowledge, that ye might be filled with all the fullness of God.

A missionary in Mexico

I prayed for six years to receive [the baptism]. I remember one pastor encouraging me that oak trees first put down deep roots and then the trunk grows to the sky. Well I prayed and I waited and I pressed through and nothing. So one day, I was taking the trash to the curb, worshipping to myself and I began to speak in another tongue. I stopped myself. There was no way that was it. The next day in church I was seated during worship time and once again I began to speak in tongues. I remember saying to the Lord if this is real please have the pastor come down and pray for me. I opened my eyes and he was coming down off the platform. First time, only time he did that for me. Pretty difficult for this "incrédulo" (unbeliever) to deny what was going on. What happened as a result? It has had a profound impact on my insight into the Scriptures. The continued experience has served as an anchor in difficult times.

A pastor in Ohio

I experienced the in filling of the Holy Spirit at a church service. Yes, hands were laid on, but I believe I was already filled on the way to the altar for prayer; I felt the warmth and began speaking in tongues on the way forward. I read scripture and prayed to prepare; I had to have my mind open and ready to receive, getting rid of unbelief, the world, and doubt.

The change for me was feeling closer and more committed to the Lord. The feeling was greater than what I experienced during salvation: more fire, belonging, and acceptance, more determined, ready to war against the enemy, and stronger in my walk. I believe speaking in tongues sealed the question of whether or not I had received the full gift; it left no question or doubt.

Howard Carter (in the Pentecostal Evangel, June 2, 1934)

The power of the Lord was surging through me. I turned round and knelt, intending to pray quietly and praise the Lord for His blessings. As I prayed the power of the Lord increased, and I soon forgot all about the meeting and was wholly taken up with the Lord. Heaven seemed wonderfully near, and the spiritual joy which flooded my being words cannot describe. I praised the Lord and rejoiced in His wonderful goodness. How long I had been on my knees I do not know, but I felt someone touch me on the arm and ask me to rise. I protested at first, fearing that the heavenly blessing would be lost, whereupon he whispered in my ear, 'You are disturbing the meeting, brother; will you come with me to the vestry, and we will pray.' I was astonished to learn that my silent prayer had become audible, and so much so that I was hindering the progress of the service. I left the seat and followed the brother into the vestry, and as I was crossing the threshold the power of the Spirit flooded me mightily. My whole being vibrated under the mighty waves of the Spirit's power which passed through me, and I broke forth for the first time in my experience in other tongues. To describe a spiritual experience is as impossible as to define the sweetness of honey, or the beauty of a flower. I may simply state that the spiritual blessing received that day met the great craving of my soul, and satisfied me that the experience for which I had yearned so long was now actually real. The Lord had granted me the gift of the Holy Spirit with the like manifestation as on the day of Pentecost and in the house of Cornelius. My heart overflowed with joy and thanksgiving and speaking with other tongues. The aching void of my Christian life was filled by the Spirit of the Lord".

A retired pastor in Florida

For me, the experience was a surprise. Susi and I were new believers, attending a New Year's Eve party with a bunch of other new believers, in Hollis Queens (in the home of a Baptist missionary). Someone suggested we get in a circle and start praying for the Baptism, so we did, and people started receiving! But not Susi or me! I started to get angry. Then, I heard the Lord tell me to get out of the circle and be by myself. I got down on my knees in a corner of the room and began to repent for anger. All of sudden something welled up inside me and burst out of my mouth. It sounded like a babbling brook! I couldn't shut it off for hours! Didn't want to! That lasted for a few days, until someone suggested I ask for a language. I did. It started and has become more precious to me in my relationship with Jesus than I can describe. Like Paul wrote, it's my spirit communicating directly with God; speaking mysteries and being built up. I have had the privilege of seeing many people in many countries come into the same delight. Tongues is my chief prayer and worship language.

I personally feel more intimate in my communion with The Lord through tongues.

Two testimonies from the Azusa Street Revival (1906)

And the power of God came upon me until I dropped to the floor. I was under the power of God for about an hour and a half, and it was there that all pride, and self, and conceit disappeared, and I was really dead to the world, for I had Christ within in His fullness. I was baptized with the Holy Ghost and spoke in a new tongue.

He finished the work on my vocal organs ... and spoke through me in unknown tongues. I arose, perfectly conscious outwardly and inwardly that I was fully baptized in the Holy Ghost, and the devil can never tempt me to doubt it. First I was conscious that a living person had come into me, and that He possessed even my physical being, in a literal sense, in so much that He could at His will take hold of my vocal organs, and speak any language He chose through me. Then I had such power on me and in me as I never had before. And last but not least, I had a depth of love and sweetness in my soul that I had never dreamed of before, and a holy calm possessed me, and a holy joy and peace, that is deep and sweet beyond any thing I ever experienced before, even in the sanctified life. And O! Such victory as He gives me all the time.

Part Two

The Holy Spirit in the Bible

Chapter 4

The Holy Spirit in the Old Testament

The Old Testament does not offer much teaching on the Spirit, and never mentions the baptism, yet it was the Bible that Jesus and the apostles knew, providing the foundational teaching for the fuller New Testament revelation. The Spirit's work in the Old Testament was limited to leaders, prophets, and those God raised up for a special purpose.

Historical books

There are about thirty-six references to the Holy Spirit in the historical books of the Old Testament, including the very first verses of the Bible:

¹In the beginning God created the heavens and the earth. ² Now the earth was formless and empty, darkness was over the surface of the deep, and the Spirit of God was hovering over the waters.

Gifts of craftsmanship

Exodus 31:1-5 records the first reference to the Spirit gifting believers for tasks in the kingdom:

Then the Lord said to Moses, "See, I have chosen Bezalel son of Uri, the son of Hur, of the tribe of Judah, and I have filled him with the Spirit of God, with wisdom, with understanding, with knowledge and with all kinds of skills— to make artistic designs for work in gold, silver and bronze, to cut and set stones, to work in wood, and to engage in all kinds of crafts.

All believers filled with the Spirit

In Numbers 11, Moses prophesied of a day when the Spirit would be poured out on all believers. On this occasion (which started with widespread complaints about a lack of meat), the Spirit that anointed Moses was passed on to the seventy elders. There is plenty of the Spirit for everyone!

[16] *The Lord said to Moses: "Bring me seventy of Israel's elders who are known to you as leaders and officials among the people. Have them come to the tent of meeting, that they may stand there with you.* [17] *I will come down and speak with you there, and I will take some of the power of the Spirit that is on you and put it on them. They will share the burden of the people with you so that you will not have to carry it alone.*

The Spirit's purpose was to equip the elders to share in Moses' work. They had to gather with him at the tent of meeting. With that obedience and expectancy, God would come down, speak with Moses, and sovereignly take some of the Spirit's power from him and put it on the elders.

[24] *So Moses went out and told the people what the Lord had said. He brought together seventy of their elders and had them stand around the tent.* [25] *Then the Lord came down in the cloud and spoke with him, and he took some of the power of the Spirit that was on him and put it on the seventy elders. When the Spirit rested on them, they prophesied—but did not do so again.*

Moses entered the tent alone, while the elders stood around it; only Moses was allowed in the glory cloud of God's presence. As God spoke to Moses, he took the Spirit and put it on the elders. The result was a visible sign of "prophesying," which we see several times in the Old Testament. Moses notes that it was a one-time experience for them—perhaps it was something he experienced regularly. It appears to be some sort of ecstatic praise.

²⁶ *However, two men, whose names were Eldad and Medad, had remained in the camp. They were listed among the elders, but did not go out to the tent. Yet the Spirit also rested on them, and they prophesied in the camp.* ²⁷ *A young man ran and told Moses, "Eldad and Medad are prophesying in the camp."*

²⁸ *Joshua son of Nun, who had been Moses' aide since youth, spoke up and said, "Moses, my lord, stop them!"*

²⁹ *But Moses replied, "Are you jealous for my sake? I wish that all the Lord's people were prophets and that the Lord would put his Spirit on them!"*

It created quite a stir that these two men (who may have rebelliously refused to join the other elders) received the Spirit and were prophesying. Joshua felt it was inappropriate! But Moses was happy and prophetically longed for a day when all God's people would have the Spirit.

Empowering for battle in Judges

In the time of the judges, one of the lowest points in Israel's history, the Spirit still came upon those God was raising up to deliver the people. The results of the Spirit's coming foreshadow what Jesus said would happen when the disciples were baptized in the Spirit.

3:10: *The Spirit of the Lord came on him, so that he became Israel's judge and went to war. The Lord gave Cushan-Rishathaim king of Aram into the hands of Othniel, who overpowered him.*

Othniel was raised up to be a leader and a conquering warrior. The Spirit equipped and empowered him.

6:34: *Then the Spirit of the Lord came on Gideon, and he blew a trumpet, summoning the Abiezrites to follow him.*

Here again, the result was leadership and empowerment for battle.

11:29: *Then the Spirit of the Lord came on Jephthah. He crossed Gilead and Manasseh, passed through Mizpah of Gilead, and from there he advanced against the Ammonites.*

Again, there is power to come against the enemy.

The remaining references in Judges are about Samson:

13:24–25: *The woman gave birth to a boy and named him Samson. He grew , and the Lord blessed him, and the Spirit of the Lord began to stir him while he was in Mahaneh Dan, between Zorah and Eshtaol.*

14:6: *The Spirit of the Lord came powerfully upon him so that he tore the lion apart with his bare hands as he might have torn a young goat.*

14:19: *Then the Spirit of the Lord came powerfully upon him. He went down to Ashkelon, struck down thirty of their men, stripped them of everything and gave their clothes to those who had explained the riddle. Burning with anger, he returned to his father's home.*

15:14: *As he approached Lehi, the Philistines came toward him shouting. The Spirit of the Lord came powerfully upon him. The ropes on his arms became like charred flax, and the bindings dropped from his hands.*

Supernatural power to overcome the enemy came with the Spirit's anointing. Do you believe the Spirit could raise you up to be a leader and defeat the enemies of God's people?

King Saul's experience in 1 Samuel

10:6 The Spirit of the Lord will come powerfully upon you, and you will prophesy with them; and you will be changed into a different person. 7 Once these signs are fulfilled, do whatever your hand finds to do, for God is with you. 9 As Saul turned to leave Samuel, God changed Saul's heart, and all these signs were fulfilled that day. 10 When he and his servant arrived at Gibeah, a procession of prophets met him; the Spirit of God came powerfully upon him, and he joined in their prophesying.

All Saul had to do was follow Samuel's instructions; the rest was God's sovereign move. Twice, it says the Spirit "powerfully" came on Saul. Certainly, it is not unusual for the Spirit to come "powerfully" on us! The purpose was to equip him to reign, transforming him into another person, changing a simple farm boy into a king. The Spirit can change you into a different person as well! Once he experienced the Spirit's filling, God would be with him in a special way, blessing whatever his hands found to do. The outpouring of the Spirit took place when he met a Spirit-filled group of prophets. While we are unsure of what is meant by their "prophesying," surely it was not each one of them speaking a prophetic message. It appears to be the same ecstatic praise we saw in Numbers, similar to the tongues we experience today.

11:4 When the messengers came to Gibeah of Saul and reported these terms to the people, they all wept aloud. 5 Just then Saul was returning from the fields, behind his oxen, and he asked, "What is wrong with everyone? Why are they weeping?" Then they repeated to him what the men of Jabesh had said.

⁶ When Saul heard their words, the Spirit of God came powerfully upon him, and he burned with anger. ⁷ He took a pair of oxen, cut them into pieces, and sent the pieces by messengers throughout Israel, proclaiming, "This is what will be done to the oxen of anyone who does not follow Saul and Samuel." Then the terror of the Lord fell on the people, and they came out together as one. ⁸ When Saul mustered them at Bezek, the men of Israel numbered three hundred thousand and those of Judah thirty thousand.

Saul did not know how to foster this newfound infilling and went back to farming, but the Spirit was still in him. When Saul heard of the threat to his people, the Spirit stirred within him. It came upon him powerfully once again (similar to the special filling of the apostles we note in Acts), and enabled Saul to take a bold step and raise a mighty army to deliver God's people from their enemy.

¹⁶:¹³ So Samuel took the horn of oil and anointed him in the presence of his brothers, and from that day on the Spirit of the Lord came powerfully upon David. Samuel then went to Ramah. ¹⁴ Now the Spirit of the Lord had departed from Saul, and an evil spirit from the Lord tormented him.

Sadly, the Spirit was so grieved by Saul's sin that he departed from Saul and was replaced by an evil spirit that tormented him. The next king (David) received the same powerful filling Saul had enjoyed, as he was anointed with oil by the prophet Samuel.

¹⁹:¹⁸ When David had fled and made his escape, he went to Samuel at Ramah and told him all that Saul had done to him. Then he and Samuel went to Naioth and stayed there. ¹⁹ Word came to Saul: "David is in Naioth at Ramah"; ²⁰ so he sent men to capture him. But when they saw a group of prophets prophesying, with Samuel standing there as their leader, the Spirit of God came on Saul's

men, and they also prophesied. ²¹ *Saul was told about it, and he sent more men, and they prophesied too. Saul sent men a third time, and they also prophesied.* ²² *Finally, he himself left for Ramah and went to the great cistern at Seku. And he asked, "Where are Samuel and David?" "Over in Naioth at Ramah," they said.* ²³ *So Saul went to Naioth at Ramah. But the Spirit of God came even on him, and he walked along prophesying until he came to Naioth.* ²⁴ *He stripped off his garments, and he too prophesied in Samuel's presence. He lay naked all that day and all that night. This is why people say, "Is Saul also among the prophets?"*

Could we have services so full of the Spirit's presence that unbelievers would fall under the power as they came in? Or could you be so full that you are on a bus praying in tongues and someone sitting next to you catches it and starts praising God in tongues? Why not? After all he had been through, Saul still spent an entire day (naked!) "prophesying" in God's presence! This must have been quite a gathering! When the Spirit is flowing, his supernatural power can take control of a person. It is not something to fear, but to enjoy.

Saul's life makes an interesting study; I have written about him in my book <u>Made to Reign</u>.

Six aspects of the Spirit's work: Isaiah 11:1–3

¹*A shoot will come up from the stump of Jesse;*
from his roots a Branch will bear fruit.
² *The Spirit of the Lord will rest on him—*
the Spirit of wisdom and of understanding,
the Spirit of counsel and of might,

the Spirit of the knowledge and fear of the Lord—
³ and he will delight in the fear of the Lord.

We know that the *"shoot"* and the *"branch"* is Jesus Christ. His life was an example of Spirit-filled living. Although he never stopped being God, he did *"empty himself"* (Phil. 2:7) and relied on the Holy Spirit for revelation, inspiration, and power to do miracles. How beautiful to have the Spirit *"rest on"* you. Even better to be baptized and wholly immersed in the Spirit!

Various aspects of the Spirit's ministry are highlighted:

- Wisdom
- Understanding
- Counsel
- Might (power)
- Knowledge
- Fear of the Lord

Are those aspects present in your life? Do they characterize the "Spirit-filled" believers and churches you are familiar with?

The Spirit physically moves you: Ezekiel 3:12-15

¹² Then the Spirit lifted me up, and I heard behind me a loud rumbling sound as the glory of the Lord rose from the place where it was standing. ¹³ It was the sound of the wings of the living creatures brushing against each other and the sound of the wheels beside them, a loud rumbling sound. ¹⁴ The Spirit then lifted me up and took me away, and I went in bitterness and in the anger of my spirit, with the strong hand of the Lord on me. ¹⁵ I came to the exiles who lived at Tel Aviv near the Kebar River. And there, where they were living, I sat among them for seven days— deeply distressed.

This was part of an amazing supernatural encounter Ezekiel had with God, so intense that it left him bitter, angry, distressed, and exhausted for days. Somehow, amidst all he was seeing, he knew it was God's Spirit who was "lifting him up" and taking him away. Do you believe the Spirit can lift you up and take you into a place of supernatural encounter with the living God?

The Spirit in us prophesied: Ezekiel 36:24–32

[24] "'For I will take you out of the nations; I will gather you from all the countries and bring you back into your own land. [25] I will sprinkle clean water on you, and you will be clean; I will cleanse you from all your impurities and from all your idols. [26] I will give you a new heart and put a new spirit in you; I will remove from you your heart of stone and give you a heart of flesh. [27] And I will put my Spirit in you and move you to follow my decrees and be careful to keep my laws.

Ezekiel prophesies a time of restoration, when God removes the heart of stone from his people, cleanses them (we know it is the blood of Jesus that cleanses us), and gives them a new heart and a new spirit. Seemingly apart from that "new spirit," he puts his Holy Spirit in them, enabling them to obey him. Rebellion and disobedience were impossible to overcome without the Spirit's power; the Spirit "moves" us to follow his decrees and gives us a desire to carefully keep his word.

The Spirit poured out on all people: Joel 2:28–29

"And afterward,
I will pour out my Spirit on all people.
Your sons and daughters will prophesy,

> *your old men will dream dreams,*
> *your young men will see visions.*
> *Even on my servants, both men and women,*
> *I will pour out my Spirit in those days."*

This is the famous prophecy Peter said was fulfilled on the day of Pentecost. The universal gift of the Spirit for all God's people is the defining experience of the latter days (Joel proceeds to talk about the end of the world). It is not *"all people"* as in every human being, but on *"my servants."* Prophecy, dreams, and visions—supernatural revelation from God—will be a feature of that outpouring. Are those things evident in your experience and your church?

The Spirit inspires the Word: Zechariah 7:12

They made their hearts as hard as flint and would not listen to the law or to the words that the Lord Almighty had sent by his Spirit through the earlier prophets. So the Lord Almighty was very angry.

This is an important Old Testament reference to the Spirit's inspiration of the Scriptures, and the Spirit as a separate but equally divine part of the Godhead.

The Old Testament primarily presents the Spirit as empowering and equipping to do God's work and defeat the enemy, while looking ahead to his widespread outpouring. Does that glimpse and taste of the Spirit in the Old Testament make you hungry for more? It should! The prophesied filling was the hallmark of the early church, and something God desires for you today!

Chapter 5

The Holy Spirit in the Gospels

John the Baptist

Luke 3:16: *John answered them all, "I baptize you with water. But one who is more powerful than I will come, the straps of whose sandals I am not worthy to untie. He will baptize you with the Holy Spirit and fire.*

John 3:16 is the famous verse on God's saving love for the world, but Luke 3:16 is equally essential. John the Baptist points to Jesus as being far greater than he was. John's primary ministry was baptism in water, whereas Jesus' work would be to baptize with the Holy Spirit. John also introduces the idea of a baptism of fire. Sometimes people separate the baptism in the Spirit from the relationship with Jesus, but it is Jesus who baptizes us! As you draw close to Jesus, you will experience more of the Spirit. It is not an either/or.

Jesus promises rivers of living water

Matthew 3:16: *As soon as Jesus was baptized, he went up out of the water. At that moment heaven was opened, and he saw the Spirit of God descending like a dove and alighting on him.*

We know John 3:16, but we just saw Luke 3:16 proclaim the baptism in the Spirit to be a key part of Jesus' ministry. Now, in

43

Matthew 3:16, we see Jesus baptized in the Spirit, an experience familiar to many who have received that baptism as they are water baptized. It would be great to see a dove alighting on you, confirming that you have received the Spirit, or tongues of fire, as at Pentecost, but that was probably more for the onlookers (or John) than for Jesus. We receive the Spirit by faith.

Luke 11:13: *If you then, though you are evil, know how to give good gifts to your children, how much more will your Father in heaven give the Holy Spirit to those who ask him!"*

God does not grudgingly give you his Spirit or make you work for it! It is a gift, a good gift that he, as a loving Father, delights to give you! He loves to see you allow the Spirit to do his work in you. All you have to do is ask him!

Luke 24:49 *"I am going to send you what my Father has promised; but stay in the city until you have been clothed with power from on high."*

Very similar to Acts 1:8, the Father promised the Spirit, Jesus sends the Spirit, and, in a slightly different perspective on the baptism, we are *clothed* with the Spirit's power. Would you say you have been clothed with that power?

John 7:37-39: *On the last and greatest day of the festival, Jesus stood and said in a loud voice, "Let anyone who is thirsty come to me and drink. Whoever believes in me, as Scripture has said, rivers of living water will flow from within them." By this he meant the Spirit, whom those who believed in him were later to receive. Up to that time the Spirit had not been given, since Jesus had not yet been glorified.*

The importance of what Jesus is about to say is emphasized by his standing (teachers customarily sat), the volume of his voice, and the fact that he waited until the last and greatest day of the festival to proclaim it. What Scripture is he referring to? Perhaps Isaiah 12:3, 43:19–20, 44:3, or 58:11. Similar to what Peter says on Pentecost, the only condition Jesus gives for receiving the Spirit is believing in him (John immediately repeats that it is for those who believe; unbelief will keep you from receiving the Spirit!). The invitation he gives is for anyone who is thirsty. We have to recognize our thirst, come to Jesus, and drink. How do we drink? It is not only to satisfy our own thirst, but as we drink of his Spirit, rivers flow from within us to bring life, healing, and his presence to everyone around us. These are rivers, not streams; not a few drops, but a flowing river, and they are not just for church leaders, but for "*whoever believes*" in Jesus. If someone came to Jesus that day at the festival, they could drink, but they would not yet experience the flowing rivers. John states that they would receive the gift later, after Jesus was glorified, which means after his resurrection, at Pentecost. Could it be that some Christians come to Jesus and drink, believe in him, but receive the Spirit later?

Jesus teaches on the Spirit in the Upper Room

John 14: *15 "If you love me, keep my commands. 16 And I will ask the Father, and he will give you another advocate to help you and be with you forever— 17 the Spirit of truth. The world cannot accept him, because it neither sees him nor knows him. But you know him, for he lives with you and will be in you. 18 I will not leave you as orphans; I will come to you.*

This is Jesus' "farewell discourse" to his disciples, but he is very clear that even though he will not be physically present with them, he will come to them, live with them, and be in them. As we see on several occasions, there is a blurring of the distinction between Jesus and the Spirit. Jesus will come to the disciples, but he comes as the Spirit.

As with most scriptural promises, there is a condition given for receiving the Spirit: Loving Jesus and keeping his commands. There is also a clear progression:

1. Obviously, we have to come into a relationship with Jesus, a love relationship.
2. How do you know if you love someone? You do what you know pleases them (as long as it also pleases God). If you love Jesus, you gladly keep his commands.
3. Then Jesus comes before the Father with a request: Give that person the Spirit.
4. As we might guess, Jesus' petitions are always granted. The Father does not evaluate if that person should receive the Spirit or not; he gives them the Spirit.

Do you think Jesus has asked the Father to give you the Spirit? Would you say you love Jesus? How are you doing with keeping his commands? Could a problem there be preventing you from receiving the Spirit? As with any gift, we have to accept it and use it. Someone could give you a beautiful gift, but if you put it on the shelf and never open it, it does you no good.

There are several things we learn about the Spirit here:

1. He is *"another advocate."* Advocate comes from the Greek word *"parakletos,"* which means "called alongside to help." The Amplified Bible follows many translations in referring to him as the Comforter, and then adds other possible translations: Counselor, Helper, Intercessor, Advocate, Strengthener, and Standby. Which of those aspects of the Spirit's work have you experienced? Is

there one that you need right now? Ask him to be that for you!

2. He is sent to help us.
3. He will never leave you—he will be with you forever (even in heaven!).
4. He is the Spirit of truth—he cannot tolerate lies; he always stands for the truth.
5. Don't be surprised if unbelievers do not understand your experience in the Spirit; the world neither sees him nor knows him, and cannot accept him. If you think about it, plenty of unbelievers talk about Jesus and God, often using their name "in vain," but you rarely hear them mention the Holy Spirit.
6. We should experience an intimate relationship with the Spirit: he is a constant companion, living in us; we can know him as profoundly as anyone can be known.

[26] But the Advocate, the Holy Spirit, whom the Father will send in my name, will teach you all things and will remind you of everything I have said to you.

Two more critical tasks of the Spirit:

1. **He will teach us all things**. However, we must be teachable, listen to him, and receive his teachings. That means spending time in God's presence without distractions, but also listening for what he may want to teach us in daily experiences and through other people.
2. **He will remind us of everything Jesus said**. That requires time in the Gospels and becoming familiar with Jesus' words, so he can then remind us of them.

Have you experienced the teaching or reminding ministry of the Spirit? Is there something you can do to be more receptive to it?

John 15: **²⁶** *"When the Advocate comes, whom I will send to you from the Father—the Spirit of truth who goes out from the Father—he will testify about me. ²⁷ And you also must testify, for you have been with me from the beginning.*

Jesus just said (14:26) that the *Father* sends the Spirit in his name; now he says that *he* will send him *from* the Father. The truth appears to be that both are anxious for us to have the Spirit. Just as there is no set way in which we receive the Spirit, there is no set way in which he is given.

Another important work of the Spirit is to testify about Jesus. This command was given to the disciples who had been with Jesus his entire ministry. Still, it is logical that if the Spirit's work is to testify about Jesus, we also must testify about him, and the Spirit will help us do that. To stay quiet will quench the Spirit.

John 16: **⁷** *But very truly I tell you, it is for your good that I am going away. Unless I go away, the Advocate will not come to you; but if I go, I will send him to you.*

How wonderful it would be to spend time with Jesus in a boat on the Sea of Galilee! Or listen to his teaching on the mountainside or in the temple courts! But here Jesus makes an astounding statement: We have something far better than his physical presence with us. Having the third person of the Trinity living inside us, providing that teaching, counsel, and comfort 24/7, is as good as it can get on this earth. In God's plan, Jesus had to leave in order to send the Spirit to us, and there is no question about the Spirit's coming; Jesus promises: *"I will send him to you."*

⁸ *When he comes, he will prove the world to be in the wrong about sin and righteousness and judgment: ⁹ about sin, because people do not believe in me; ¹⁰ about righteousness, because I am going* *to the Father, where you can see me no longer;* [11] *and about judgment, because the prince of this world now stands condemned.*

The Spirit powerfully works in the world around us, not only in believers. Whether the person is a believer or not, it is not our job to convict. There are three areas in which the Holy Spirit convicts, far better than we can:

1. **Sin**. Unbelief is a sin. Sin is not only evil deeds, but the refusal to believe in Jesus. The Holy Spirit can convict of that sin and also open the eyes and hearts of unbelievers to see the truth and believe.
2. **Righteousness**. Jesus' resurrection and ascension confirm his righteousness. Our righteousness does not depend on our good works, but on Christ's work on the cross. The Spirit creates a longing for righteousness, convicts us of our unrighteousness, and leads us to receive Jesus' righteousness.
3. **Judgment**. Satan already stands condemned, a stark reminder that the days of his evil influence in this world are limited, and judgment will surely come to those who persist in their unbelief and unrighteousness. It can be discouraging to see "the prince of this world" seemingly free to steal, kill, and destroy, but his condemnation was secured at the cross.

[12] *"I have much more to say to you, more than you can now bear.* [13] *But when he, the Spirit of truth, comes, he will guide you into all the truth. He will not speak on his own; he will speak only what he hears, and he will tell you what is yet to come.* [14] *He will glorify me because it is from me that he will receive what he will make known to you.* [15] *All that belongs to the Father is mine. That*

is why I said the Spirit will receive from me what he will make known to you."

If Jesus said he could only do what he saw his Father do and say what the Father gave him to say, that is even truer of the Spirit. If it is an authentic work of the Spirit, he does not draw attention to himself, but glorifies Jesus. He is attentive to what Jesus says, and faithfully passes that on to us. There is a clear flow of authority and ministry: The Father is the source, and shares everything he has with Jesus. The Spirit does not act on his own initiative, but takes what he receives from Jesus and makes it known to us:

1. **He will guide us into all truth**. He is the Spirit of truth. We can expect "much more" revelation of Jesus' heart through the ministry of the Spirit. They will be deep things, more than what the disciples could handle at that point.

2. **He will tell us what is yet to come**. There are many conflicting voices about what that will be! God wants us to know what is coming, but there is a great need to listen carefully to the Spirit and discern what is true.

John 20:21–22: *Again Jesus said, "Peace be with you! As the Father has sent me, I am sending you." And with that he breathed on them and said, "Receive the Holy Spirit.*

Every born-again believer has the Spirit dwelling in them (Rom. 8:9). At first glance, Jesus breathing on them and sending them out seems to fulfill the promise of the Spirit and power, but then he told them to wait to go until they were clothed with power from on high. We may experience the breath of God on us and even have experience in the Spirit, but not be baptized in the Spirit.

God is in the "sending" business. We tend not to stay in the same place, but go where God can use us. Receiving the Spirit often results in being sent; resisting God's call can quench the Spirit. A willingness to be sent and preparation to go may result in Jesus "breathing" on us and giving us the Spirit. The disciples had much to learn and experience about the Spirit, but they had the promise and had to wait on God until they received it. You have the promise. Have you received it? The book of Acts tells us what happened.

Chapter 6

Experiences of the Baptism in the Book of Acts

This book, which is formally called "The Acts of the Apostles," has often been nicknamed "The Acts of the Holy Spirit," since the Spirit is so central in it. For a fuller study of all the Spirit's work in Acts, read the fourth book in my series "*Walk Like Jesus Walked*," Receive the Power.

Jesus' promise and the purpose: Acts 1

⁴ On one occasion, while he was eating with them, he gave them this command: "Do not leave Jerusalem, but wait for the gift my Father promised, which you have heard me speak about. ⁵ For John baptized with water, but in a few days you will be baptized with the Holy Spirit."

⁸ You will receive power when the Holy Spirit comes on you; and you will be my witnesses in Jerusalem, and in all Judea and Samaria, and to the ends of the earth."

Jesus very specifically spoke of a baptism with the Holy Spirit, comparing it to and differentiating it from John's baptism in water. We saw very few references to it in the Gospels, but Jesus says they had heard him speak about it; he may have shared

53

many things with them that were not recorded. It is a gift that the Father wants to give every believer, a promised gift. They were commanded to wait until they received it; God would sovereignly pour it out, clothe them, fill them, and immerse them in it, just as repentant sinners were immersed in water.

What would they receive in the baptism? Power! The very power of Almighty God dwells in them. Power to overcome sin and walk in obedience to Christ; specifically, power to be witnesses in worldwide outreach. The natural result of receiving the baptism should be power and a vibrant witness, accompanied by a concern for the nations. If you feel powerless and lack concern for the unsaved, you probably need to question if you have been baptized in the Spirit.

Pentecost: Acts 2

[1]When the day of Pentecost came, they were all together in one place. [2] Suddenly a sound like the blowing of a violent wind came from heaven and filled the whole house where they were sitting. [3] They saw what seemed to be tongues of fire that separated and came to rest on each of them. [4] All of them were filled with the Holy Spirit and began to speak in other tongues as the Spirit enabled them.

Finally, the promise is dramatically fulfilled! It was a sovereign, supernatural work of God. There was no question about whether this was it; when you are baptized in the Spirit, you know it! They were "*all together*," the "*whole house*" was filled, the tongues of fire rested on "*each of them*," "*all of them were filled*" with the Spirit, and "*all of them*" spoke in tongues, enabled by the Spirit. God does not want anyone to miss out on this experience! We may receive the baptism alone, but the Spirit works most freely in a united body of believers, as Jesus said in Matthew 18:20:

"Where two or three are gathered in my name, there am I in the midst of them."

Can we expect a violent wind and tongues of fire? There is no reason it could not happen again, but it probably won't. This was a very special initial outpouring of the Spirit, which was intended in part to draw the attention of the crowds gathered in Jerusalem.

⁵ Now there were staying in Jerusalem God-fearing Jews from every nation under heaven. ⁶ When they heard this sound, a crowd came together in bewilderment, because each one heard their own language being spoken. ⁷ Utterly amazed, they asked: "Aren't all these who are speaking Galileans? ⁸ Then how is it that each of us hears them in our native language? ⁹ Parthians, Medes and Elamites; residents of Mesopotamia, Judea and Cappadocia, Pontus and Asia, ¹⁰ Phrygia and Pamphylia, Egypt and the parts of Libya near Cyrene; visitors from Rome ¹¹ (both Jews and converts to Judaism); Cretans and Arabs—we hear them declaring the wonders of God in our own tongues!" ¹² Amazed and perplexed, they asked one another, "What does this mean?" ¹³ Some, however, made fun of them and said, "They have had too much wine."

Many have said that the disciples were speaking known languages, from all the countries mentioned, but I believe there were two miracles that day: in the believers' tongues, and in the ears of the crowd. Three times it says *"we hear them speak;"* that is why they were bewildered and amazed! A simple experiment will confirm it: Take 120 people, speaking loud enough to attract a crowd. Fifteen distinct groups are mentioned here; if 120 people are speaking fifteen languages at the same time, nothing could be understood. God did a miracle of translation for each person!

After the anointed preaching, the people ask what they must do, and Peter replied:

[38] *"Repent and be baptized, every one of you, in the name of Jesus Christ for the forgiveness of your sins. And you will receive the gift of the Holy Spirit."*

Peter makes clear that this marvelous experience is not only for the apostles, but for every believer, as he just quoted from Joel's prophecy. They must repent, be cleansed of their sins, and be baptized. Then they *will receive* the gift of the Spirit. Surely God wants the same for you.

Everyone filled: Acts 4

[31] *After they prayed, the place where they were meeting was shaken. And they were all filled with the Holy Spirit and spoke the word of God boldly.*

These believers had already been baptized in the Spirit, but as we have noted, there can be repeated fillings. Once again, the context was a gathering of believers praying together. Just like Pentecost, they were *all filled*. The result was boldness in speaking God's word, probably primarily testifying to unbelievers.

Samaria receives the Spirit: Acts 8

[14] *When the apostles in Jerusalem heard that Samaria had accepted the word of God, they sent Peter and John to Samaria.* [15] *When they arrived, they prayed for the new believers there that they might receive the Holy Spirit,* [16] *because the Holy Spirit had not yet come on any of them; they had simply been baptized in the name of the Lord Jesus.* [17] *Then Peter and John placed their hands on them, and they received the Holy Spirit.*

This was a significant step in the spread of the Gospel (even though, after Jesus' encounter with the Samaritan woman in John 4, many had trusted in him). Philip, one of the deacons designated in Acts 6, brought the Gospel to Samaria in the persecution and dispersion that followed Stephen's martyrdom.

- Many believed in Jesus and were baptized.
- There was a problem with the baptism, however: They were only baptized in the name of Jesus. Philip had not been present when Jesus gave the Great Commission and the Trinitarian formula for baptism. They were not rebaptized, but there is an evident link between correct baptism and receiving the Holy Spirit, as Peter preached on the day of Pentecost. This verse presents a real problem for the "Jesus only" people who say that the only way to baptize is "in Jesus' name only."
- When they arrived, it was immediately evident to Peter and John that they had not received the Holy Spirit. They should have; that was the norm. It doesn't specify how they knew, but their priority was to correct it. Can you imagine doing that when you visit a church?
- Peter and John prayed for them, laid hands on them, and (presumably) they all received the Spirit.

No mention is made of tongues, but there was something visible that happened when the apostles laid hands on them that caught the attention of a magician living in Samaria:

[18] When Simon saw that the Spirit was given at the laying on of the apostles' hands, he offered them money.

Saul receives the Spirit: Acts 9

[17] Then Ananias went to the house and entered it. Placing his hands on Saul, he said, "Brother Saul, the Lord—Jesus, who

appeared to you on the road as you were coming here—has sent me so that you may see again and be filled with the Holy Spirit." ¹⁸ Immediately, something like scales fell from Saul's eyes, and he could see again. He got up and was baptized, ¹⁹ and after taking some food, he regained his strength.

Although we know Paul was baptized in the Spirit and spoke in tongues, no mention is made of that at his conversion. Jesus does not tell Ananias to pray for the Spirit to fill Saul, but Ananias says the dual purpose of his visit was the healing of his sight and the filling of the Spirit. Someone needed to pray for that. We are never told that he was filled; he was healed, baptized, ate, and regained his strength. Most likely, he was filled with the Spirit at that point. If Jesus sent you to someone to pray for the infilling of the Spirit, would you be sensitive to his leading?

The Spirit falls on Cornelius' household: Acts 10

⁴⁴ *While Peter was still speaking these words, the Holy Spirit came on all who heard the message. ⁴⁵ The circumcised believers who had come with Peter were astonished that the gift of the Holy Spirit had been poured out even on Gentiles. ⁴⁶ For they heard them speaking in tongues and praising God.*

Then Peter said, ⁴⁷ "Surely no one can stand in the way of their being baptized with water. They have received the Holy Spirit just as we have." ⁴⁸ So he ordered that they be baptized in the name of Jesus Christ. Then they asked Peter to stay with them for a few days.

We have seen the Spirit come sovereignly, and also with the laying on of hands. In Samaria, they believed, but were baptized in the Spirit later. Here, the power of God was so present, Peter's anointing was so great, and the people were so receptive, that the Spirit came on the whole crowd before Peter could finish his sermon, give an invitation, or pray for them. How did they know that this was the same outpouring of the gift of the Spirit? They were speaking in tongues and praising God. It was evident that it was the same experience as Pentecost. Here, Spirit baptism preceded water baptism, but Peter immediately ministers the water baptism as well.

Peter recounts to a skeptical church what happened: Acts 11

[15] *"As I began to speak, the Holy Spirit came on them as he had come on us at the beginning.* [16] *Then I remembered what the Lord had said: 'John baptized with water, but you will be baptized with the Holy Spirit.'* [17] *So if God gave them the same gift he gave us who believed in the Lord Jesus Christ, who was I to think that I could stand in God's way?"*

As Peter explained how Gentiles were now part of the church, the confirming sign was the baptism in the Spirit, just as the Spirit had come upon them at Pentecost. No mention is made of tongues, although we know from chapter 10 that they spoke in tongues, and most likely his audience knew that when the Spirit comes on us *"as he had come on us at the beginning,"* it would include tongues.

Did you receive the Spirit when you believed? Acts 19

Paul had not met Apollos and was unaware of his ministry in Ephesus. He did find the fruit of his labors: a small group of disciples. But, oddly, Paul immediately sensed that something was wrong:

¹*While Apollos was at Corinth, Paul took the road through the interior and arrived at Ephesus. There he found some disciples* ²*and asked them, "Did you receive the Holy Spirit when you believed?"*

They answered, "No, we have not even heard that there is a Holy Spirit."

³*So Paul asked, "Then what baptism did you receive?"*

"John's baptism," they replied.

⁴*Paul said, "John's baptism was a baptism of repentance. He told the people to believe in the one coming after him, that is, in Jesus."* ⁵*On hearing this, they were baptized in the name of the Lord Jesus.* ⁶*When Paul placed his hands on them, the Holy Spirit came on them, and they spoke in tongues and prophesied.* ⁷*There were about twelve men in all.*

The Lord may have revealed it to him, but most likely, Paul noticed something lacking among these disciples: There was no power or manifestations of the Holy Spirit. He expected that when you believe in Jesus, you receive the Spirit. That was usually the case in Acts. Someone would accept Jesus, be baptized in water, and at the same time be baptized in the Spirit, usually accompanied by speaking in tongues. However, that was not always the case, as we see now in Ephesus. Before he could do any further ministry, Paul's priority was correcting this. Here, the issue was simple ignorance: they had never even heard of the Holy Spirit. Ignorance of the Spirit is not uncommon today, either.

It is essential to follow Paul's thinking: When he found out that they did not know about the Spirit, his first thought was, "There must have been some problem with their baptism." For Paul, there was an intimate connection between water and Spirit baptism. If they had been baptized, they should have had the Spirit. However, it is even possible to be baptized—in ignorance—and not receive everything the Lord has for you. They had only been baptized in John's baptism, a baptism of repentance.

When we follow the New Testament model, we should experience similar results:

1. They were baptized in water.
2. Paul laid hands on them. There is power in the laying on of hands, and God often uses it to impart the Holy Spirit.
3. The Holy Spirit came on them.
4. They spoke in tongues and prophesied. The coming of the Spirit is almost always accompanied by some proclamation from our mouths: praise, new tongues, and, in this case, prophecy (probably more closely resembling the ecstatic prophesying spoken of in the Old Testament than giving prophetic messages).

Did you receive the Holy Spirit when you believed? If you are not sure, are you open to whatever the Lord might do to give you that necessary power?

Chapter 7

The Holy Spirit in Romans

5:5: *And hope does not disappoint us, because God's love has been poured out into our hearts through the Holy Spirit, who has been given to us.*

Paul's focus in the fifth chapter is the certainty of our hope. How can we be so sure? The very thing we read in so many testimonies that people experienced in their Spirit baptism: love! God's love, poured out into our hearts as a gift from the Father! Would you say you have experienced that? Are you aware that many Christians are unsure of God's love for them? The fullness of the Spirit is pure love! Have you received your gift? Do you have that assurance of a living hope for the future?

8:5–16: Paul has left the despair of Romans 7, where he continually fails to do the right thing under the law, and rejoices in the deliverance and victory that is available through Jesus. But how does that work? First, he says we are free of condemnation (8:1) because *"through Christ Jesus the law of the Spirit who gives life has set you free from the law of sin and death"* (8:2). Amazingly, he says that the righteous requirements of the law are met in those who live according to the Spirit. Clearly, the Holy Spirit plays a critical role in the Christian life. How? He starts by comparing and contrasting those who live in the flesh and those who live in the Spirit:

⁵ *Those who live according to the flesh have their minds set on what the flesh desires; but those who live in accordance with the Spirit have their minds set on what the Spirit desires. ⁶ The mind governed by the flesh is death, but the mind governed by the Spirit is life and peace. ⁷ The mind governed by the flesh is hostile to God; it does not submit to God's law, nor can it do so. ⁸ Those who are in the realm of the flesh cannot please God.*

If you live according to the flesh:

- You have your mind set on what the flesh desires.
- Your mind, which is governed or ruled by your flesh, is death.
- Your mind is hostile to God.
- It does not submit to God's law.
- It is unable to submit to that law; it is powerless to do so.
- You cannot please God.

I am sure you know what your flesh desires. Notice how fleshly living starts in the mind, in your thoughts. Your flesh rules over your mind, which then directs your actions. This was Paul's experience in the past, and unfortunately, the experience of many "Christians." Although some describe this person as a "carnal Christian," we will see in a moment that there is no such thing; they are not saved.

If you live by the Spirit (the Spirit-filled life):

- Your mind is set on what the Spirit desires.
- The Spirit-governed mind is life and peace.

What does the Spirit desire? What do you find yourself thinking about most of the time? Are you experiencing life and peace? If you find that you are more controlled by the flesh, how can you change that?

⁹ You, however, are not in the realm of the flesh but are in the realm of the Spirit, if indeed the Spirit of God lives in you. And if anyone does not have the Spirit of Christ, they do not belong to Christ. ¹⁰ But if Christ is in you, then even though your body is subject to death because of sin, the Spirit gives life because of righteousness. ¹¹ And if the Spirit of him who raised Jesus from the dead is living in you, he who raised Christ from the dead will also give life to your mortal bodies because of his Spirit who lives in you.

Verse 9 makes it clear: If you belong to Christ, if you are saved, you have his Spirit (notice that first he says the *"Spirit of God"* and a moment later the *"Spirit of Christ;"* there is tremendous unity among the three persons, and this is another confirmation of Christ's divinity). If God's Spirit lives in you, he is powerful enough that your life is *"in the Spirit"* and should be controlled by the Spirit. Does that mean there are no fleshly temptations? No! The body is still subject to death because of sin, but there should be a powerful presence of life in you since the same Spirit who raised Jesus from the dead lives in you and gives you life.

¹² Therefore, brothers and sisters, we have an obligation—but it is not to the flesh, to live according to it. ¹³ For if you live according to the flesh, you will die; but if by the Spirit you put to death the misdeeds of the body, you will live.

Again, Paul concedes that our flesh will cause us to sin, but now we have a way of dealing with it: *"By the Spirit"* we put those misdeeds to death. He is writing to Christians, but he is concerned that some might be living *"according to the flesh."* If they do, they will not be saved; they will die. The Christian is obligated to live according to the Spirit. Though he speaks of the Spirit controlling our minds, we do not lose our free will, but can grieve and quench the Spirit by our sinful choices.

How do you go about putting the body's misdeeds to death? Taking them to the cross, crucifying them, repenting of the sin, and allowing the Spirit to fill your mind and thoughts.

14 For those who are led by the Spirit of God are the children of God. 15 The Spirit you received does not make you slaves, so that you live in fear again; rather, the Spirit you received brought about your adoption to sonship. And by him we cry, "Abba, Father." 16 The Spirit himself testifies with our spirit that we are God's children.

Unlike the law, with its rigidity and ugly penalties, the Spirit of God leads us and confirms in our hearts that we have been adopted as God's sons and daughters. If you feel like a slave in your church or live in fear, there is something wrong; that is not the Holy Spirit at work. He is gentle, bringing the Father's love and guidance into your life and fostering an intimate relationship with him.

8:26-27: *26 In the same way, the Spirit helps us in our weakness. We do not know what we ought to pray for, but the Spirit himself intercedes for us through wordless groans. 27 And he who searches our hearts knows the mind of the Spirit, because the Spirit intercedes for God's people in accordance with the will of God.*

Do you ever struggle in your prayer life? Are there times you don't know what to pray for? No problem! Paul struggled too! But that is precisely why God gives us his Spirit; he searches our hearts, knows our needs, and intercedes for us. His prayer is always in accordance with God's will, which means it always gets answered. Here, Paul speaks of groans too deep for words. Have you ever prayed like that? Prayer in tongues is part of the help that the Spirit offers, as he prays through us in an angelic language.

14:17-18: *For the kingdom of God is not a matter of eating and drinking, but of righteousness, peace and joy in the Holy Spirit, because anyone who serves Christ in this way is pleasing to God and receives human approval.*

Many Christians and church leaders appear to be intent on establishing a "kingdom" on earth through political power, massive organizations, media presence, and influential churches. As much as people like to eat in some churches, you might think the kingdom was about food and drink! Paul was probably referring to legalistic rules regarding kosher regulations or other prohibitions on food and drink. The kingdom is not about any of those material concerns, but rather about a life full of the Holy Spirit. That is the place where God truly reigns, and it is necessarily a corporate experience, because a "kingdom" does not consist of just you! You are part of a *"kingdom of priests"* (Rev. 1:6).

Life in the Spirit should be characterized by righteousness (a holy life that honors God), peace (interior, with God, and with others; free of anxiety and stress), and joy (so much for the rigid, legalistic, dour experience of some believers!). It is also a life of service! We do not experience the Spirit just to feel good and be blessed, or even for a nice social experience in church. We serve Christ, not out of obligation or anxiety, but expressing the righteousness, peace, and joy which the Spirit gives us. That is the service that pleases God and which others, even those antagonistic to the Gospel, find hard to denounce. We walk without reproach; much as others try to find some fault in us, they cannot, and thus we receive human approval, which, contrary to what some Christians think, is important to God!

15:13: *May the God of hope fill you with all joy and peace as you trust in him, so that you may overflow with hope by the power of the Holy Spirit.*

God's love is "poured out into our hearts" by the Spirit, which affirms our hope. We just saw that life in the Spirit involves righteousness, peace, and joy. Now Paul says that as a result of our faith and trust in the God of hope, he *fills* us with *all* joy and peace. This is not just an occasional taste in a worship service, but a total filling. How does that happen? Through the power of the Holy Spirit! It takes that divine power to overcome the heaviness of life in this world and its problems, which often leaves us hopeless. But the Spirit is so powerful in us that we *overflow* with hope. What a tremendous gift!

I have to add one note of concern here as I reflect on Paul's heart. This great apostle does not "declare" that they are filled with joy and peace; he does not have that power, even as an anointed servant of God. He *asks* God to fill them. Being full of the Spirit does not give us the right to "declare" things that God sovereignly does.

Chapter 8

The Holy Spirit in the Other Epistles

1 Corinthians

2:4: *My message and my preaching were not with wise and persuasive words, but with a demonstration of the Spirit's power.*

We have repeatedly seen that the Spirit empowers us. Paul acknowledged that he was not an impressive preacher—he confessed that he did not use wise or persuasive words! What about preachers who seek to entertain, impress, manipulate, and persuade people? We see too few true demonstrations of the Spirit's power in today's preaching! To demonstrate that power, we must be filled with the Spirit and focused on the Spirit-inspired Scripture, putting self aside and letting the Spirit speak through us.

2:9–14: *However, as it is written:*

"What no eye has seen,
what no ear has heard,
and what no human mind has conceived"—
the things God has prepared for those who love him—

these are the things God has revealed to us by his Spirit.

The Spirit searches all things, even the deep things of God. For who knows a person's thoughts except their own spirit within them? In the same way no one knows the thoughts of God except the Spirit of God. What we have received is not the spirit of the world, but the Spirit who is from God, so that we may understand what God has freely given us. This is what we speak, not in words taught us by human wisdom but in words taught by the Spirit, explaining spiritual realities with Spirit-taught words. The person without the Spirit does not accept the things that come from the Spirit of God but considers them foolishness, and cannot understand them because they are discerned only through the Spirit.

- The Spirit is revelatory. If we do not have that relationship with the Spirit, there is no way we can understand the fullness of what God has prepared for us—either now, or for eternity. You can expect to receive insight into that when you allow the Spirit to work in you, and take the time to wait on him for the revelation.
- The Spirit knows the very depths of God's thoughts. He searches God's heart, and our hearts, exposing and revealing what is in them. The Spirit knows God's thoughts, and gives us glimpses of them as we live in his fullness.
- Only the Spirit can enable us to truly understand what God has freely given us.
- These things are so supernatural that the Spirit must teach us how to communicate them adequately. You can expect that kind of teaching ability when you allow the Spirit to give you the right words.
- You may have struggled in the past to accept some things about the baptism in the Holy Spirit or the Gospel, many

of which seem like foolishness to the world. Once you receive the Spirit, suddenly they all make sense.

3:16: *Don't you know that you yourselves are God's temple and that God's Spirit dwells in you?*

6:19: *Do you not know that your bodies are temples of the Holy Spirit, who is in you, whom you have received from God?*

Two parallel references to the sanctity of the human body. Far from being evil or mere flesh, your body is the temple of the Holy Spirit. We do not worship our bodies—something all too common, even among Christians—but we care for them, exercise them, nourish them with healthy food, and avoid anything that would damage that temple, such as tobacco, alcohol, or drugs. The context in chapter 6 is on holiness in our sexual lives. Remember, the Spirit dwells in you; your body is his temple.

2 Corinthians

1:21–22: *[God] anointed us, set his seal of ownership on us, and put his Spirit in our hearts as a deposit, guaranteeing what is to come.*

We have great security and assurance in our relationship with Christ. Ephesians states that it is the Spirit who puts that seal on us. He anoints us, and his seal of ownership lets the principalities and powers know that we belong to God. The deposit of the Spirit in our hearts is a guarantee of heaven. Do you have assurance that you belong to God? The baptism of the Spirit brings an unshakable conviction that a glorious future awaits you in God's presence.

3:17-18: *Now the Lord is the Spirit, and where the Spirit of the Lord is, there is freedom. And we all, who with unveiled faces contemplate the Lord's glory, are being transformed into his image with ever-increasing glory, which comes from the Lord, who is the Spirit.*

The Spirit breaks all the bondage in your life. Wherever the Spirit is in his fullness, there should be no bondage or legalism, but freedom to love, to worship, and to serve God. If you feel restricted in those areas, you, your church, or those closest to you may need to be set free by this baptism.

When was the last time you would say you contemplated the Lord's glory? Does your life reflect ever-increasing glory? Or has the glow of God's glory dimmed over the years?

Part of the Spirit's work is to transform you into God's image, which may involve some painful "surgery" and crucifixion of the flesh. The focus on Spirit baptism emerged from the holiness tradition of a "second blessing" of sanctification. Indeed, there can be a dramatic advance in our conformity to God's image when we receive the baptism. Still, Paul says this is an ongoing work of transformation, which comes as we contemplate God's glory and give his Spirit the freedom to work in our lives. Do not resist what God is trying to do! Too many Christians contemplate the screens of their TV, computer, and cell phone, instead of taking the time to contemplate God's glory. It is more rewarding than whatever you are seeing on that screen!

Galatians

3:2-5: *I would like to learn just one thing from you: Did you receive the Spirit by the works of the law, or by believing what you heard? Are you so foolish? After beginning by means of the Spirit, are you now trying to finish by means of the flesh? Have you experienced so much in vain—if it really was in vain? So again I ask, does God give you his Spirit and work miracles among you by the works of the law, or by your believing what you heard?*

Faith is essential to receive the Spirit. You must believe that he exists and that it is God's plan to gloriously fill you with him. Hopefully, this book has strengthened your faith and increased your expectancy of receiving this blessing. Cultures and churches that have that faith and expect God to come and work miracles experience that supernatural work. Although there may be things you need to repent of to prepare for the Spirit, you cannot be "good enough" to deserve the baptism, or follow some prescription that makes God pour out his Spirit on you.

The Galatians started well, allowing the Holy Spirit to work in them, but they got religious and lost that initial fervor. Paul says it is possible to experience the blessings of the Spirit in vain if we turn back to religion, trying to be good enough and doing things our way. Too many Christians are foolish, attempting to finish God's work by their own efforts. Are you like the Galatians?

5:16-18: *So I say, walk by the Spirit, and you will not gratify the desires of the flesh. For the flesh desires what is contrary to the Spirit, and the Spirit what is contrary to the flesh. They are in conflict with each other, so that you are not to do whatever you want. But if you are led by the Spirit, you are not under the law.*

Many Christians experience an initial burst of power and victory over sin when they receive the baptism, but they allow things into their lives that keep them from experiencing the Spirit's fullness. They may not have been taught that beyond the emotion and the initial blessing of the baptism, there is a daily walk of faith in his power that enables you to resist the desires of the flesh. Have you made accommodation to the flesh over time? Do you even recognize the difference between what the flesh desires and what the Spirit desires? Are you aware of that inner conflict?

This is a promise: *Walk by the Spirit and you will not gratify the desires of the flesh.* Make sure that throughout the day, every day, you are led by the Spirit. His paths are far better than yours! He wants to lead you! If you fall back into being guided by what your flesh wants, you put yourself under the law, and are obligated to obey all of it. Ask God daily to help you walk in the Spirit.

5:22-25: *But the fruit of the Spirit is love, joy, peace, forbearance, kindness,   goodness,   faithfulness, gentleness   and   self-control. Against such things there is no law. Those who belong to Christ Jesus have crucified the flesh with its passions and desires. Since we live by the Spirit, let us keep in step with the Spirit.*

Are you experiencing more of the flesh or the Spirit? The previous verses talk about the works of the flesh. Now he presents the fruit of the Spirit. These are not things you can work at to make part of your life; they are the natural results of allowing the Spirit to fill you. How much are you experiencing them right now? Is the Spirit being allowed to grow and manifest himself in your life? Or are your "*passions and desires*" choking off the good fruit the Spirit wants to produce in you?

Part of initially receiving Christ and being baptized is genuine repentance from sin, crucifying the flesh and its passions. As we receive the Spirit's fullness, we walk by the Spirit, live by the Spirit, and keep in step with the Spirit. Christ is the center of our lives. The Spirit fills us not only in church or when we are doing some ministry for Christ, but all the time. Are you keeping in step with the Spirit? Or are you totally out of sync with him?

6:8: *Whoever sows to please their flesh, from the flesh will reap destruction; whoever sows to please the Spirit, from the Spirit will reap eternal life.*

These are decisions you make throughout the day. They may not be blatant sins, but, at any point, you may be sowing to please the flesh or sowing to please the Spirit. That glimpse of pornography sows powerful seeds to your flesh, but it does not have to be that blatant. It can be the choice between a secular radio station and a station playing worship music. The spiritual law is that when you sow enough to the flesh, you will surely reap destruction. Think back on decisions you have made over the past few days. Are you sowing more to the flesh, or to the Spirit? Have you been reaping some bad fruit?

Ephesians

1:13–14: *And you also were included in Christ when you heard the message of truth, the gospel of your salvation. When you believed, you were marked in him with a seal, the promised Holy Spirit, who is a deposit guaranteeing our inheritance until the redemption of those who are God's possession—to the praise of his glory.*

Some have argued that teaching a baptism in the Spirit separate from conversion implies that we do not believe the Spirit is already in our lives. This Scripture makes clear that when you believe, you are marked with that seal of the promised Holy Spirit. You have the deposit, the guarantee, that you are God's possession. Perhaps we can view the baptism as the next installment and overflow of the deposit you received when you believed.

3:16–17: *I pray that out of his glorious riches he may strengthen you with power through his Spirit in your inner being, so that Christ may dwell in your hearts through faith.*

Here is the power of the Spirit again, at work in your inner being. And here is that vague distinction we have noted previously: is it the Spirit or is it Christ who dwells in your heart? It is the Spirit of Christ! It may not be possible (or necessary) to make an absolute distinction! What is impressive is that, out of God's infinite riches, his Spirit strengthens us with supernatural power! Who does not want or need that?

Once again, Paul does not "declare" this for them, but prays that God would do it.

4:30: *And do not grieve the Holy Spirit of God, with whom you were sealed for the day of redemption.*

Another reference to the seal of the Spirit, and the alarming possibility of grieving this Spirit, who is such a blessing to us! Why would anyone want to do that? We usually do not do it consciously, but rather through little sins, disobedience, or crowding him out. Eventually, we grieve him to the point that we have to come back and be "baptized" all over again, after repenting of the sin that has grieved him.

5:18-20: *Do not get drunk on wine, which leads to debauchery. Instead, be filled with the Spirit, speaking to one another with psalms, hymns, and songs from the Spirit. Sing and make music from your heart to the Lord, always giving thanks to God the Father for everything, in the name of our Lord Jesus Christ.*

As on the day of Pentecost, the filling of the Holy Spirit can be so powerful that you appear to be drunk. This is a command: *Be filled with the Spirit.* God gives the Spirit, but there are things we must do to allow him freedom to work in us. There are several ways given here to do that:

- Fellowship with other believers. We are full of the Spirit and God's love, and cannot keep it to ourselves, but are drawn to other believers. It is hard to maintain the fullness of the Spirit alone.

- A big part of that is worship. Three aspects of worship are given: the speaking and singing of Scripture (especially the Psalms), hymns that have been written in praise to God, and songs the Spirit gives (the spontaneous singing I mentioned in chapter two as lacking in many churches today).
- Worship from the heart when alone, with songs we already know, and *"making music"* with Spirit-inspired songs. That is hard to do with the constant presence of the media, music on the cell phone, and noise around us.
- Having a thankful heart. Consciously give thanks to God for everything. A grumbling, complaining heart quenches the Spirit.

6:17–18: *Take the helmet of salvation and the sword of the Spirit, which is the word of God. And pray in the Spirit on all occasions with all kinds of prayers and requests.*

Two more important ways we can sow to the Spirit and be filled with him:

- The Spirit has given us a sword to use in the daily battles of life: The Bible. We must study it, meditate on it, and memorize it so that we can use it as a sword. You will find that as Scripture fills your thoughts, your conversation, and your heart, you will experience more of the Spirit's fullness.
- As Paul makes clear in 1 Corinthians 14, praying in the Spirit is praying in tongues. The more you pray in tongues, the more you will experience the Spirit's fullness. You can pray in tongues all day long. Try it. Whether in English or in tongues, that communion and connection with God is essential to maintaining the

Spirit's fullness, and you will find his fruit overflowing in your life!

1 Thessalonians

5:19–20: *Do not quench the Spirit; do not treat prophecies with contempt.*

We can *grieve* the Spirit; now we see it is also possible to *quench* the Spirit. It may not be blatant sin, but too much of the good things of the world (sports, music, TV, internet, work) can result in ignoring the Spirit and quenching him.

We can also quench the Spirit by treating his ministries and manifestations with contempt. Prophecy is specified here. Many churches quench the Spirit in their services by not allowing manifestations of his gifts.

Titus

3:5-6: *He saved us through the washing of rebirth and renewal by the Holy Spirit, whom he poured out on us generously through Jesus Christ our Savior.*

How are we saved? By the washing of our sins as we repent and are born again, symbolized by baptism in water, and the ongoing renewal by the Holy Spirit—not just by a few drops, but a baptism, as the Spirit is generously poured out on us.

Hebrews

10:29: *How much more severely do you think someone deserves to be punished who has trampled the Son of God underfoot, who has treated as an unholy thing the blood of the covenant that sanctified them, and who has insulted the Spirit of grace?*

We can grieve, quench, and, now, insult the Holy Spirit. How? By blatant, conscious sin, which treats the blood of Jesus with contempt.

1 John

3:24; 4:13: *And this is how we know that he lives in us: We know it by the Spirit he gave us. This is how we know that we live in him and he in us: He has given us of his Spirit.*

The Spirit's presence in your life is a daily reminder that you live in Christ and he lives in you.

Jude

20: *But you, dear friends, build yourselves up in your most holy faith and pray in the Holy Spirit.*

Two commands:

1. Build yourself up in your faith, probably primarily in fellowship, and hearing, studying, and meditating on the Word, since faith comes by hearing and hearing by the Word of God.
2. Praying in tongues, as the New Testament equates praying in the Spirit with praying in tongues. Paul states in 1 Corinthians 14 that the person who prays in tongues edifies himself, and that is what Jude is telling us to do here.

Part Three

The Holy Spirit in You

Chapter 9

A Spirit-filled Church

As the Spirit fills each believer, gifts are given to equip the church for ministry. First Corinthians 12 gives us the clearest teaching of how the church functions.

You are the body of Christ

²⁷ Now you are the body of Christ, and each one of you is a part of it.

Can a church function without the baptism of the Holy Spirit? This may sound radical, but I would have to say no. The Holy Spirit plays a critical role in the proper functioning of the Body of Christ. It is not a social club or religious organization, nor is it something you choose to join. When you accept Jesus into your life, you become a part of his body. It is very hard to be a true Christian alone—our faith involves a relationship with God and other believers. Jesus no longer walks this earth, but his body is everywhere. Miraculously, there are millions of local expressions of Christ's body all over the world. If they follow God's plan, with each member in its place manifesting gifts of the Holy Spirit, each church can do what Jesus did.

¹² Just as a body, though one, has many parts, but all its many parts form one body, so it is with Christ. ¹³ For we were all baptized by one Spirit so as to form one body—whether Jews or Gentiles, slave or free—and we were all given the one Spirit to drink. ¹⁴ Even so the body is not made up of one part but of many.

Drinking of the Spirit and being baptized in the Spirit are not just for the super-spiritual or fanatics. Twice we are told that this fullness of the Spirit is for every Christian: we were *"all baptized"* and *"all given the one Spirit to drink."* Unity flows from our common experience of the Holy Spirit, in baptism (in the Spirit, water, or both), and drinking of his fullness. The Spirit is like water, the essential life force. The body will not function if everyone is not drinking of the Spirit.

God uses something each of us is intimately familiar with to help us understand the unity and diversity of the church: our bodies. For your body to function correctly, every member must do its part, working together with the other members. There would be chaos if they did not obey the head (your brain), or, in the church, Jesus Christ. Jesus' blood (spiritually) flows through his whole body, purifying it and bringing nutrients to each member.

Absolute equality in the body

There is no difference between black and white, rich and poor, or powerful and humble. The Spirit erases all those divisions in a bond of love. Any prejudice is sin, which destroys the church and grieves its Lord.

[15] Now if the foot should say, "Because I am not a hand, I do not belong to the body," it would not for that reason stop being part of the body. [16] And if the ear should say, "Because I am not an eye, I do not belong to the body," it would not for that reason stop being part of the body. [17] If the whole body were an eye, where would the sense of hearing be? If the whole body were an ear, where would the sense of smell be? [18] But in fact God has placed the parts in the body, every one of them, just as he wanted them to be. [19] If they were all one part, where would the body be? [20] As it is, there are many parts, but one body.

Just as your foot cannot decide it is tired of being stepped on all the time, you cannot simply decide you no longer want to be part of Christ's body. Rebellion is not allowed. Unfortunately, all the hands tend to gather in one place, all the feet in another—and on it goes, resulting in a dysfunctional, deformed body. Contrary to what Paul says about us needing each other, hands often feel they are better than feet and do not need them, so we end up with cripples who cannot walk and certainly do not reflect the glorious presence of Jesus Christ. We must accept all the gifts and the many expressions of the body, and discern where God wishes to place the members. Questioning how he has placed the members is tantamount to saying God does not know how to build a church.

21 The eye cannot say to the hand, "I don't need you!" And the head cannot say to the feet, "I don't need you!" 22 On the contrary, those parts of the body that seem to be weaker are indispensable, 23 and the parts that we think are less honorable we treat with special honor. And the parts that are unpresentable are treated with special modesty, 24 while our presentable parts need no special treatment. But God has put the body together, giving greater honor to the parts that lacked it, 25 so that there should be no division in the body, but that its parts should have equal concern for each other. 26 If one part suffers, every part suffers with it; if one part is honored, every part rejoices with it.

This is common sense, but, unfortunately, many Christians fail to grasp the importance of this simple teaching. If you have ever hurt your foot, you know it impacts your whole life. Each part of our bodies has a vital function; none is more important than the others. There is amazing coordination among the various parts, but if they start fighting each other, your body will break down. Are you familiar with autoimmune diseases, where your body's defenses attack your own body? What a shame that it afflicts the body of Christ! Each member should show genuine concern for the other members, recognizing their unique value. If we allow God to put the body together as he wants it, division should be rare.

The Spirit imparts gifts in the context of the body

[1]*Now about the gifts of the Spirit, brothers and sisters, I do not want you to be uninformed or misinformed.*

Unfortunately, many Christians are both. What is a spiritual gift? It is simply a *manifestation of the Spirit* (v. 7). A gift has nothing to do with your natural talents; it is God supernaturally working through your life, for the benefit of his church. If you are quenching the Spirit, denying his power, or full of yourself instead of the Spirit, he cannot manifest himself. If your church tries to control the Spirit or does not expect anything supernatural, gifts probably will not be manifest.

Gifts are supernatural abilities that you cannot perform in your own strength. When "spiritual gift inventories" are completed, hardly anyone ends up with "miraculous" gifts. If you believe those inventories, there would be a significant imbalance in the body. I suspect that much that passes for "gifts" is natural talent.

Often, someone will possess complementary gifts, such as healing through the word of knowledge or faith, accompanied by miracles. I do not see biblical evidence that the gifts become our "possession," so that we necessarily operate in the same gift for life. That may often be the case, but since it is the Spirit's manifestation, it could change according to the needs of the church.

*⁴ There are different kinds of gifts, but the **same Spirit** distributes them. ⁵ There are different kinds of service, but the **same Lord**. ⁶ There are different kinds of working, but in all of them and in everyone it is the **same God** at work.*

Unity in diversity

We can expect significant differences in the way Spirit-filled congregations look and work. The Trinity demonstrates what God intends for the church: perfect unity, but with diverse functions. In these three verses, Paul parallels the Holy Spirit, the Lord Jesus, and God the Father, confirming the divinity and equality of each member of the Trinity.

⁷ Now to each one the manifestation of the Spirit is given for the common good. ⁸ To one there is given through the Spirit a message of wisdom, to another a message of knowledge by means of the same Spirit, ⁹ to another faith by the same Spirit, to another gifts of healing by that one Spirit, ¹⁰ to another miraculous powers, to another prophecy, to another distinguishing between spirits, to another speaking in different kinds of tongues, and to still another the interpretation of tongues. ¹¹ All these are the work of one and the same Spirit, and he distributes them to each one, just as he determines.

Though there is great diversity in the gifts, they all flow from one source, the Holy Spirit. Verse one of chapter 14 tells us to desire gifts and even seek certain gifts. The last verse of chapter 12 says: *Now eagerly desire the greater gifts* (v. 31), yet it is still the Spirit who determines what you receive. He knows what the church needs, he knows you completely, and he distributes the gifts perfectly, just as he wants.

²⁸ And God has placed in the church first of all apostles, second prophets, third teachers, then miracles, then gifts of healing, of helping, of guidance, and of different kinds of tongues. [29] Are all apostles? Are all prophets? Are all teachers? Do all work miracles? [30] Do all have gifts of healing? Do all speak in tongues? Do all interpret? [31] Now eagerly desire the greater gifts.

The leadership of the church is presented in the context of the gifts the Spirit distributes. Without the work of the Spirit, we can have a capable CEO or administrator leading the church, but we will not have the order and anointing that God requires for the body to function correctly.

There is a hierarchy of gifts; Paul mentions *greater gifts.*

- Apostles are in first place, as a foundation for the church.
- Prophets follow. What a shame that many churches do not recognize these two foundational gifts! Is it any surprise the church is weak?
- Paul does not mention evangelists or pastors, though they are part of the five ministry offices in Ephesians four. Here, he puts teachers in third place, followed by those who work miracles.

We need to submit to God, gratefully accepting whatever gift he gives us. Do not envy those with *"greater gifts."* The obvious answer to the question "Does everyone have certain gifts?" is "No." The same Spirit is at work, but there is great diversity in the gifts.

If we are to function as Christ intended us to, we need all these manifestations of the Spirit. Open your heart for the Lord to speak to you about gifts in your life and church. With something so important, I am confident he will guide you if you are genuinely open.

Chapter 10

Tongues

As you have seen in the testimonies, the baptism of the Spirit and speaking in tongues are the same thing for many people. So much so that some Pentecostal denominations have stated that tongues are the essential sign of the baptism. In the Acts accounts we studied, tongues are usually present. It certainly seems desirable, and indeed Paul wrote: "*I would like every one of you to speak in tongues*" (1 Cor. 14:5). So why has tongues been so controversial? Perhaps because it seems strange, and those who do not speak in tongues have been made to feel like second-class Christians, while those who have it may have misused it or overemphasized it.

Almost all the negative talk about tongues comes from those who do not have it. Some claim that 1 Corinthians 13:8 says that tongues (and prophecy) ceased when "perfection" (in their minds, the New Testament) came. And yet, it is clear from the context that "perfection" refers to when we see Jesus face to face; few would argue that we have arrived at perfection now. And if tongues have ceased, what about the millions of sincere believers who speak in tongues? They point to other religions that supposedly speak in tongues, or say it is of the devil, but that denies what the scripture says and what the fruit in the lives of tongues-speakers confirms.

It is a very minor biblical doctrine to cause such an uproar. The Old Testament never mentions it, although we have seen an interesting connection between tongues and prophecy (cf. Acts 19:6, and the Old Testament references to prophesying when the Spirit fell, Num. 11:25–27 and 1 Sam. 10:5–13; 18:10 and 19:20–24). It appears to be an ecstatic praise similar to tongues, because it is clear they were not proclaiming messages received from the Lord.

Jesus never spoke about tongues in the Gospels, except in the so-called "disputed" ending of Mark (16:17) where it is included along with deliverance and healing as a sign that will accompany belief in Jesus. Outside of Acts, the only time tongues is mentioned in the New Testament is in First Corinthians, bringing correction to a church that over-emphasized tongues.

Paul said in chapter 12 that not everyone speaks in tongues (v. 30), yet that contradicts what I just quoted him saying in chapter 14. Although it is not clearly defined in Scripture, it is evident that the gift spoken of in chapter 12 is for use in the church (along with the gift of interpretation) to bring a message from the Lord. That is distinct from the experience on Pentecost or the other Acts accounts where they all spoke in tongues, or the "prayer language" or "tongue of angels" Paul talks about in chapter 14.

Tongues in 1 Corinthians 14

²For anyone who speaks in a tongue does not speak to people but to God. Indeed, no one understands them; they utter mysteries by the Spirit.

When you pray in tongues, the third person of the Trinity dwelling in your heart communicates directly with the Lord. They may be mysteries, but many times I have a sense of what I am praying about. This is a great advantage in prayer, as you are always praying God's will and can intercede for the needs of your family and others who are far away.

⁴ Anyone who speaks in a tongue edifies themselves, but the one who prophesies edifies the church. ⁵I would like every one of you to speak in tongues, but I would rather have you prophesy. The one who prophesies is greater than the one who speaks in tongues, unless someone interprets, so that the church may be edified.

The advantage of prophecy is that it blesses the whole church, but there is nothing wrong with edifying yourself! Far from making it self-centered and worthless (as some have claimed), it is an amazing God-given provision to build yourself up in the Spirit any time!

¹⁴For if I pray in a tongue, my spirit prays, but my mind is unfruitful. ¹⁵So what shall I do? I will pray with my spirit, but I will also pray with my understanding; I will sing with my spirit, but I will also sing with my understanding.

These verses suggest that when the New Testament refers to praying in the Spirit, it means praying in tongues. It is important to pray with your understanding (in English), but also to pray and sing in tongues. Tongues serve as the oil that gets the Spirit flowing in your life.

Tongues are primarily for private use

⁶Now, brothers and sisters, if I come to you and speak in tongues, what good will I be to you, unless I bring you some revelation or knowledge or prophecy or word of instruction? ⁷Even in the case of lifeless things that make sounds, such as the pipe or harp, how will anyone know what tune is being played unless there is a distinction in the notes? ⁸Again, if the trumpet does not sound a clear call, who will get ready for battle? ⁹So it is with you. Unless you speak intelligible words with your tongue, how will anyone know what you are saying? You will just be speaking into the air.

10Undoubtedly there are all sorts of languages in the world, yet none of them is without meaning. 11If then I do not grasp the meaning of what someone is saying, I am a foreigner to the speaker, and the speaker is a foreigner to me. 12So it is with you. Since you are eager for gifts of the Spirit, try to excel in those that build up the church.

16Otherwise when you are praising God in the Spirit, how can someone else, who is now put in the position of an inquirer, say "Amen" to your thanksgiving, since they do not know what you are saying? 17You are giving thanks well enough, but no one else is edified.

19But in the church I would rather speak five intelligible words to instruct others than ten thousand words in a tongue.

Paul spends significant time emphasizing the superiority of prophecy because it edifies the whole church. But he has just described the benefits of tongues, so he certainly is not belittling them. Somehow, the Corinthians had become overly focused on speaking in tongues during services, rather than focusing on what would edify the entire church.

20Brothers and sisters, stop thinking like children. In regard to evil be infants, but in your thinking be adults. 21In the Law it is written: "With other tongues and through the lips of foreigners I will speak to this people, but even then they will not listen to me, says the Lord."

To finish this thought, Paul quotes Isaiah, saying that even the gift of tongues would not touch a hardened heart. It is a sign of immaturity to be overly focused on tongues—"stop thinking like children".

Guidance on the use of tongues

I thank God that I speak in tongues more than all of you (v. 18).

If you have an angelic prayer language, use it! I have talked with elderly saints who proudly say: "Praise God! Thirty years ago, the Lord baptized me in the Spirit, and I spoke in tongues," but they have never spoken in tongues since! They never developed the gift. It is easy to forget tongues' primary purpose (helping you pray and edifying yourself) when the focus is on tongues as a sign.

Nobody will care if you walk down the street praying (quietly) in tongues. I do it a lot. They will think you are from another country or talking on your cell phone! If I go several days without speaking in tongues, I have to check what is going on in my spirit, because I have noticed a direct relationship to my spiritual health. When I am walking in the Spirit, I pray in tongues a lot.

If God has given you this gift, you can start speaking in tongues whenever you want to. You do not have to wait for some special feeling or an anointed service. If you are starting out, you may find yourself repeating the same word and wonder if you are making it up. Like a baby learning to talk, you start simply, but with practice, your tongues become more fluent. Sadly, many people never bother to develop it.

So if the whole church comes together and everyone speaks in tongues, and inquirers or unbelievers come in, will they not say that you are out of your mind? (v. 23)

A service where everyone is yelling out in tongues does not impress anyone, especially not God. It can be a stumbling block to those who are not used to tongues, and confirms unbelievers' suspicion that Christians (especially of the Pentecostal/Charismatic bent) are crazy. In church, pray or worship in tongues so that no one else hears it.

For this reason the one who speaks in a tongue should pray that they may interpret what they say (v. 13).

If anyone speaks in a tongue, two—or at the most three—should speak, one at a time, and someone must interpret. If there is no interpreter, the speaker should keep quiet in the church and speak to himself and to God (vv. 27–28).

There is a difference between public interpreted tongues (which function like prophecy) and the private prayer language. If someone is in the habit of speaking out in tongues without interpretation, a leader should talk to them. Unfortunately, some people like to draw attention to themselves and discredit the genuine gift. If a message is given in tongues, pray for interpretation, and wait for God to provide it. It is helpful to explain to the church what is happening, especially for those who are not accustomed to speaking in tongues.

Therefore, my brothers and sisters, be eager to prophesy, and do not forbid speaking in tongues (v. 39).

Churches that forbid tongues are in sin. Sound, biblical teaching on tongues is rare, but much needed. If you have already spoken in tongues but no longer use it, I pray this is a spark the Spirit would use to stir up the gift.

Is tongues the sign of Spirit baptism?

At Pentecost, all of them were filled and all of them spoke in tongues. Based on what happened there, some insist that genuine tongues are foreign languages. God obviously can give someone knowledge of a language they never learned; I have heard of that happening. But aside from the fact that Paul says tongues are mysteries that no one can understand, there are several reasons I believe the tongues on Pentecost were not foreign languages:

- Four times it says the crowd *heard* them speaking in their own language. This was a double miracle, where God effectively provided translation to the hearers. That is why they were bewildered, amazed, and perplexed.

- 120 people were speaking loud enough to draw a crowd, and fifteen people groups were mentioned. A simple experiment with that many people loudly speaking that many languages will show that no one would have been able to understand anything.

- The disciples were acting and speaking in such a way that others thought they were drunk.

There were two other instances where they all spoke in tongues: In Acts 10:45–46 it was tongues that convinced the Jews that they had received the Spirit, and in Acts 19:6, when Paul placed his hands on them, the Holy Spirit came on them, and they spoke in tongues and prophesied. In the only other record of receiving the baptism, in Acts 8:17, it could be tongues that attracted Simon's attention, though they are not mentioned.

Are three out of four events enough to form a doctrine that tongues must be the sign of Spirit baptism? Scripture never teaches that, although it is safe to say the result of baptism in the Spirit is speaking forth God's praises, usually in tongues, and when it was received, everyone experienced it. To make it *the sign*, however, seems to go against 1 Corinthians 14:22: *Tongues, then, are a sign, not for believers but for unbelievers.*

Chapter 11

How can you stay full of the Spirit?

Hopefully you are convinced from the Scriptures we have studied that the Holy Spirit dwelling within you is central to God's plan for you as a Christian. All of God's infinite power is available to help you experience it. Jesus was the only one who had ever experienced the Spirit without measure:

For the one whom God has sent speaks the words of God, for God gives him the Spirit without limit (Jn. 3:34).

What Jesus did, he did through the power of the same Spirit that indwells you. His life is an example of the Spirit-filled life for you to follow. Our human weaknesses, sin, and ignorance limit our experience. The Spirit-filled life is definitely at odds with most of our experience. We will examine several ways you can encourage the Spirit, but we will begin with the trio that constantly works against the Spirit.

The world, the flesh, and the devil

The world cannot understand the Spirit. While they may be OK with you going to church and listening to inspiring messages, when you start talking about tongues and the Spirit guiding you, they will call you a fanatic and look at you funny—even family members. Then we have our flesh to deal with. It demands to be satisfied, and the world encourages us to "meet our needs." It is so much easier to sit down with some junk food and watch a movie when you come home from work than to dedicate an hour to communion with Jesus or go to church. We can waste hours watching nothing on YouTube, and all that content on TV and the internet serves to awaken fleshly appetites. On top of that is the devil. If this is as central to the Christian life as we are saying it is, he will do everything he can to keep you from experiencing the fullness of the Spirit. The on-fire Christian who walks like Jesus and witnesses to everyone around him is a significant threat to the devil! He does not care that much if you go to church, enjoy the music, and have fun times with other believers. But when you get serious about Spirit-filled living, he will try his best to distract you and defeat you.

The Holy Spirit teaches you how to resist this trio and empowers you to do so. He will lead you into victorious spiritual battles over these enemies. These are some ways you can combat that trio and encourage a consistent walk in the Spirit:

Obey

When God sees that you are listening and available, he will give you many ministry opportunities, as we see in the stories of Phillip and the Ethiopian eunuch in Acts 8, and Ananias and Saul in Acts 9. God will test you with small steps of obedience, and as you develop the habit of obeying, he will entrust you with larger tasks.

Make it a habit to put into practice what you are reading in Scripture and hearing in church. John Stott pointed out in his book Baptism and Fullness that one of the key things he has observed keeping people from experiencing the Spirit's fullness is their knowledge outstripping their obedience. That may explain why new believers or those newly baptized in the Spirit have such a dynamic walk with the Lord: They eagerly grasp onto everything they hear or read and put it into practice. As we spend more time in church, conferences, and watching preachers, we get an information overload. There is just way too much to put into practice. Daily personal Scripture reading, asking God to show you one thing to do that day, and weekly feeding from your pastor, receiving one primary focus to work on that week, is probably all we can handle.

When we consciously disobey (which is sin) or ignore what God is telling us to do, we quench the Spirit.

Abide

Jesus discusses the importance of abiding in him in John 15. That connection with Christ throughout the day is critical to maintaining the Spirit's fullness. A couple of hours on Sunday and fifteen minutes of prayer in the morning or at night will not do it. A consistent devotional life of Scripture, worship, and prayer is the foundation for abiding.

Witness

One of the primary purposes of the Spirit is to empower you to evangelize. You will feel the Spirit's presence when you witness to someone and God gives you the words to say, and the thrill of seeing them accept Christ and have their life transformed. God will almost invariably give you opportunities to witness after you have been baptized in the Spirit. If you choose to ignore them, you will quench the Spirit. If you get comfortable with an enjoyable experience in church and retreat from the "front lines," you will lose the dynamic of the Spirit's presence. Ask yourself: Am I doing something I can only do through the Spirit's empowering? Or can I handle what I am doing in my own strength? Stepping out in faith will release the Spirit's power.

Allow the gifts to manifest

God distributes at least one gift for the benefit of the church to every Spirit-filled believer. As you identify and operate in that gift, the Spirit will flow through you. He is given for a purpose: reaching the world for Christ, building up the church, and empowering you to live for Jesus. It is not primarily about good feelings and having an uplifting time in church, although those things usually happen. There will be times when the feelings are gone, and it is time to operate in faith, knowing that the Spirit is with you and will use you as you allow that gift and calling to manifest.

Sow to the Spirit

As we saw in Galatians 6, you constantly have a chance to sow to the flesh or the Spirit. As you go through the day and make choices about what to do, ask: Is this sowing to my flesh or to the Spirit? You may not feel like going to church, but when you choose to go, you are sowing to the Spirit. The alternative might not be bad: it could be sleeping in, working out, or going to the beach. But when you choose that over something that sows to the Spirit, you are sowing to your flesh. The same with what you watch on TV or the music you listen to. A lot of secular music sows thoughts to your flesh or brings back memories of your past. You can choose to listen to music that focuses on Jesus, and sow to the Spirit. Set your mind on the things of the Spirit.

Be involved in a church of like-minded believers

Some Spirit-baptized believers are led to stay in a "dead" church to bring the life of the Spirit there, but generally, you need a church that believes in the supernatural work of the Spirit and expects manifestations of his gifts; a church that reflects the first-century church as the New Testament describes it. There should be inspired preaching/teaching of the Word, worship that draws you into God's presence, encouragement to evangelize and be involved in missions, a godly leader with a true pastor's heart, and spiritually encouraging fellowship.

Quenching and grieving the Spirit

Problems in any of the above areas will serve to quench or grieve the Spirit. When you do that long enough, you will lose the fullness of the Spirit. Learn to listen to his still, small voice. Pay attention to that gentle nudge that you should not be watching something, going somewhere, or doing something. Sin grieves the Spirit, and habitual sin will quench the Spirit. Ask yourself as you are considering something: Will this make the Spirit happy, or grieve him?

Chapter 12

Have you received the baptism?

Hopefully you are hungry at this point for more of the Spirit. You should never get to the point where you are bored as a Christian or feel you have gotten it all. There is always more! Are you one of these?

- You have been a Christian for a while but never understood (or heard of) the baptism in the Holy Spirit. You are ready to receive it.
- You felt the baptism and tongues were not for today, perhaps even looked down on Pentecostals. You can see you missed out on a beautiful gift from God.
- You were baptized in the Spirit years ago, but have allowed various things to quench the Spirit's fullness. You are eager for a fresh baptism.
- You have sought the baptism for a long time, but felt you never received it. You may be part of a Pentecostal/Charismatic church, and look with some envy on others who have received the baptism. Now you have renewed faith and a sense of expectancy that God wants it for you.
- You realize you are not saved. You are a religious church-goer, but have missed out on the riches of the Christian life.

As we have seen in the testimonies, there is no single way God imparts this gift. It is his sovereign, supernatural work. We cannot force him to do anything, and we certainly do not want to manipulate emotions or manifestations to make people think they have received it when they have not. These are some ways to prepare yourself to receive it:

1. **Make sure you are saved**. Many people from mainline and Catholic churches who received the baptism during the height of the renewal were probably being born again for the first time. To receive the baptism, first you must enter a saving relationship with Jesus Christ, following him, accepting his forgiveness, and acknowledging him as Lord of your life. If you are unsure that you have made that step, you can pray this prayer right now:

> *Lord Jesus, I believe you are the Son of God who died on the cross and rose again. I confess that I am a sinner, and without you, I am destined for an eternity in hell. I believe you paid for my sins by your death and shed blood. Forgive me and save me. I repent of my sin and sincerely want to follow you. I place you on the throne as my Lord. I surrender to you and give you control of my life. I receive you as my Lord and Savior. Thank you for saving me.*

Be sure that Jesus is truly your Lord; that you have given him complete control of your life.

2. **Confess all sin, and genuinely repent of your sin**. He is the **Holy** Spirit, and will not feel welcome if there is sin in your life. The Spirit is the one who convicts of sin, so ask him to show you if there is sin you may be unaware of; confess it, and give thanks to Jesus for his sacrifice, which paid the price of your sin. We are not perfect; we all probably sin daily, but you should feel grieved for your sin and run to Jesus asking his forgiveness. Be assured, he will forgive you:

This is the message we have heard from him and declare to you: God is light; in him there is no darkness at all. If we claim to have fellowship with him and yet walk in the darkness, we lie and do not live out the truth. But if we walk in the light, as he is in the light, we have fellowship with one another, and the blood of Jesus, his Son, purifies us from all sin.

If we claim to be without sin, we deceive ourselves and the truth is not in us. If we confess our sins, he is faithful and just and will forgive us our sins and purify us from all unrighteousness. If we claim we have not sinned, we make him out to be a liar and his word is not in us.

My dear children, I write this to you so that you will not sin. But if anybody does sin, we have an advocate with the Father—Jesus Christ, the Righteous One. He is the atoning sacrifice for our sins, and not only for ours but also for the sins of the whole world (1 Jn. 1:5–2:2).

If you are practicing sin with an unrepentant heart, you probably will not experience the baptism.

3. **Study and pray through the booklet "*Have you made the wonderful discovery of the Spirit-filled Life?*" in Appendix 1**. Although it does not talk about tongues or use the term "baptism in the Spirit," there is excellent teaching on the basics of the Spirit-filled life.

4. **If you have not been baptized in water as a believer, do so**. Peter promised on the day of Pentecost that if you repent and are baptized, you will receive the Spirit. In Acts 8, Spirit baptism accompanied water baptism, and this seems to be the pattern. Ideally, there will be a prayer for the baptism of the Spirit at the same time you are baptized in water.

5. **Study the Scriptures and come to a firm belief that the baptism in the Spirit is biblical and is something God wants for you.** If you have doubts about it, you probably will not receive it. Approach God with an expectancy and faith that you will receive:

> *Did you receive the Spirit by the works of the law, or by believing what you heard?* (Gal. 3:2)

> *"If you then, though you are evil, know how to give good gifts to your children, how much more will your Father in heaven give the Holy Spirit to those who ask him!"* (Jesus, in Lk. 11:13)

6. **Expect to speak in tongues.** Though we cannot say definitively that tongues are the sign of the baptism, as you have seen in the testimonies and the study of the Scriptures, tongues are an important part of the baptism for most people. I see no reason why God would not want to bless you with that prayer language. There is no need to manipulate it (you want it to be real!), but come to God with expectancy that you will receive it. Tell him you desire more intimate communication. Give your tongue to the Lord. Some find it hard to let go of the feeling that it is weird, or they don't need it, or don't want to be fanatical. If that is you, confess it to the Lord. Those who look down on "tongues-speakers" and insist they will never speak in tongues are probably the ones who truly need it as a point of surrender to the Lord. Typically, there is a welling up from your heart and into your throat that fills your mouth and will express itself in a new language. Open your mouth and say whatever comes out. Sometimes it is good to start with sighs or *"groans too deep for words"* (Rom. 8:26), allowing yourself to deeply breathe in the Spirit, and breathe out whatever words he may give you. Do not be surprised or discouraged if it sounds silly at first. Keep practicing and allow the language to develop.

7. **Spend time with God**. In the old days, Pentecostal churches would have "tarrying" services, where people might spend hours waiting on God to be filled with the Spirit. This is his timetable, not ours. It could be a worship service at church or worship alone at home, in a place where you will be undisturbed and can pour your heart out in worship and prayer to God.

8. **Ask**. If you do not receive it immediately, keep asking until you do: *Then Jesus told his disciples a parable to show them that they should always pray and not give up. He said: "In a certain town, there was a judge who neither feared God nor cared what people thought. And there was a widow in that town who kept coming to him with the plea, 'Grant me justice against my adversary.' "For some time he refused. But finally he said to himself, 'Even though I don't fear God or care what people think, yet because this widow keeps bothering me, I will see that she gets justice, so that she won't eventually come and attack me!'"*

And the Lord said, "Listen to what the unjust judge says. And will not God bring about justice for his chosen ones, who cry out to him day and night? Will he keep putting them off? I tell you, he will see that they get justice, and quickly (Lk. 18:1–8).

9. **Have someone who has received the baptism lay hands on you and pray**. Several scriptural examples include the laying on of hands.

10. **Get involved in a church that encourages the fullness of the Spirit and manifestations of his gifts**. That can be very important after receiving the baptism as well, to maintain and grow in your walk in the Spirit.

Here is a prayer to get you started on the Spirit-filled life:

Jesus, I believe you are the Son of God who lived on this earth, died on the cross, rose from the dead, and reigns with the Father in heaven. I acknowledge you as my Lord and Savior, and ask you to cleanse me from all sin and prepare me to receive your promised Holy Spirit. Thank you for this amazing provision. I believe you want to fill me and empower me. Just like the disciples in the Upper Room on the day of Pentecost, I am praying and waiting on you in expectancy. I believe that one ministry of the Spirit is a prayer language, and I ask that you would fill my mouth with a new tongue. I need you, Holy Spirit of God, to guide, counsel, comfort, teach, and empower me. Baptize me, fill me completely. Take control of my life. Give me spiritual gifts according to your plan, and power to witness for you. Help me never to grieve you or quench your work in my life. Thank you for filling me, in Jesus' Name.

Start worshipping and thanking Jesus for his work in your life, and take time to allow the Spirit to fill you and work in you.

Conclusion

If you have reached this point in the book, chances are the words "baptism in the Spirit," "Pentecostal," and "tongues" have not turned you off, stereotyped me, or shut your heart to the message. The exact terminology is not important. What happened to you ten or twenty years ago is not that important. God is sovereign and able to work in many ways. Do not get hung up on tongues. Prayerfully reflect on the Scriptures and the teaching of this book. It should be very clear: You need the Holy Spirit, God wants to give you the Holy Spirit, and you can always experience more of the Spirit. It does not matter so much what you call it; the important thing is to walk in the fullness of the Spirit now. I am one of many people who have experienced multiple "baptisms" or infillings. It may be what your spirit is longing for right now. Let him fill your life. Now more than ever, we need all God has intended for us in the Spirit-filled life.

Appendix 1

Have You Made the Wonderful Discovery of the Spirit-Filled Life?

Dr. Bill Bright

Every day can be an exciting adventure for the Christian who knows the reality of being filled with the Holy Spirit and who lives constantly, moment by moment, under His gracious direction.

THREE TYPES OF PEOPLE

1. Natural Person (Self-Directed Life)

(Someone who has not received Christ.)

111

Self is on the throne, directing decisions and actions (represented by the dots), often resulting in frustration. Jesus is outside the life.

"A natural man does not accept the things of the Spirit of God; for they are foolishness to him, and he cannot understand them, because they are spiritually appraised" (1 Corinthians 2:14).

2. Spiritual Person (Christ-Directed Life)

(One who is directed and empowered by the Holy Spirit.)

Jesus is in the life and on the throne. Self is yielding to Jesus. The person sees Jesus' influence and direction in their life.

"He who is spiritual appraises all things...We have the mind of Christ" (1 Corinthians 2:15).

3. Carnal Person (Self-Directed Life)

(One who has received Christ, but who lives in defeat because he is trying to live the Christian life in his own strength.)

Jesus is in the life but not on the throne. Self is on the throne, directing decisions and actions (represented by the dots), often resulting in frustration.

"And I brethren, could not speak to you as to spiritual men, but as to carnal men, as to babes in Christ. I gave you milk to drink, not solid food; for you were not yet able to receive it. Indeed, even now you are not yet able, for you are still carnal. For since there is jealousy and strife among you, are you not fleshy, and are you not walking like mere men?" (1 Corinthians 3:1-3)

THE PROMISE & THE PROBLEM

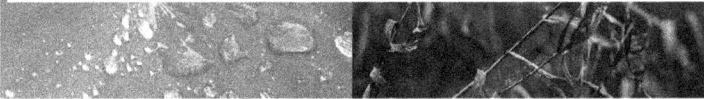

God has promised and provided for us an abundant and fruitful Christian life.

Jesus said, "I came that they might have life, and might have it abundantly" (John 10:10).

"I am the vine, you are the branches; he who abides in Me, and I in him, he bears much fruit; for apart from Me you can do nothing" (John 15:5).

"But the fruit of the spirit is love, joy, peace, patience, kindness, goodness, faithfulness, gentleness, self-control; against such things there is no law" (Galatians 5:22, 23).

"But you shall receive power when the Holy Spirit has come upon you; and shall be My witnesses both in Jerusalem, and in all Judea and Samaria, and even to the remotest part of the earth" (Acts 1:8).

The Spiritual Person

Some spiritual traits which result from trusting God:

- Christ-centered
- Empowered by the Holy Spirit
- Introduces others to Christ
- Effective prayer life
- Understands God's Word
- Trusts & obeys God
- Experiences love, joy, peace, patience, kindness, faithfulness, gentleness, goodness & self-control

The degree to which these traits are manifested in the life depends upon the extent to which the Christian trusts the Lord with every detail of his life, and upon his maturity in Christ. One who is only beginning to understand the ministry of the Holy Spirit should not be discouraged if he is not as fruitful as more mature

Christians who have known and experienced this truth for a longer period.

Why is it that most Christians are not experiencing the abundant life?

Carnal Christians cannot experience the abundant and fruitful Christian life. The carnal person trusts in his own efforts to live the Christian life:

1. He is either uninformed about, or has forgotten, God's love, forgiveness, and power (Romans 5:8-10; Hebrews 10:1-25; 1 John 1; 2:1-3; 2 Peter 1:9; Acts 1:8).
2. He has an up-and-down spiritual experience.
3. He cannot understand himself - he wants to do what is right, but cannot.
4. He fails to draw upon the power of the Holy Spirit to live the Christian life.
   (1 Corinthians 3:1-3; Romans 7:15-24; 8:7; Galatians 5:16-18)

The Carnal Person

Some or all of the following traits may characterize the Christian who does not fully trust God:

- Unbelief
- Disobedience

- Poor prayer life
- No desire for Bible study
- Legalistic attitude or critical spirit
- Impure thoughts, jealousy, guilt
- Frustration, aimlessness
- Worry, discouragement
- Loss of love for God and others

(The individual who professes to be a Christian but who continues to practice sin should realize that he may not be a Christian at all, according to 1 John 2:3; 3:6, 9; Ephesians 5:5).

THE SOLUTION

Jesus promised the abundant and fruitful life as the result of being filled (directed and empowered) by the Holy Spirit.

The Spirit-filled life is the Christ-directed life by which Christ lives His life in and through us in the power of the Holy Spirit (John 15).

1. One becomes a Christian through the ministry of the Holy Spirit, according to John 3:1-8. From the moment of spiritual birth, the Christian is indwelt by the Holy Spirit at all times (John 1:12; Colossians 2:9, 10; John 14:16, 17). Though all Christians are indwelt by the Holy Spirit, not all

Christians are filled (directed and empowered) by the Holy Spirit.

2. The Holy Spirit is the source of the overflowing life (John 7:37-39).
3. The Holy Spirit came to glorify Christ (John 16:1-15). When one is filled with the Holy Spirit, he is a true disciple of Christ.
4. In His last command before His ascension, Christ promised the power of the Holy Spirit to enable us to be witnesses for Him (Acts 1:1-9).

How, then, can one be filled with the Holy Spirit?

We are filled by the Holy Spirit by faith; then we can experience the abundant and fruitful life which Christ promised to each Christian.

You can appropriate the filling of the Holy Spirit right now if you:

1. Sincerely desire to be directed and empowered by the Holy Spirit (Matthew 5:6; John 7:37-39).
2. Confess your sins. By faith thank God that He has forgiven all of your sins – past, present and future – because Christ died for you (Colossians 2:13-15; 1 John 1; 2:1-3; Hebrews 10:1-17).
3. Present every area of your life to God (Romans 12:1, 2).
4. By faith claim the fullness of the Holy Spirit, according to:
   o **His Command:** Be filled with the Spirit. "And do not get drunk with wine, for that is dissipation, but be filled with the Spirit" (Ephesians 5:18).

○ **His Promise:** He will always answer when we pray according to His will. "And this is the confidence which we have before Him, that, if we ask anything according to His will, He hears us. And if we know that He hears us in whatever we ask, we know that we have the requests which we have asked of Him" (1 John 5:14, 15).

Faith can be expressed through prayer...

How to pray in faith to be filled with the Holy Spirit

We are filled with the Holy Spirit by faith alone. However, true prayer is one way of expressing your faith. The following is a suggested prayer:

"Dear Father, I need You. I acknowledge that I have been directing my own life and that, as a result, I have sinned against You. I thank You that You have forgiven my sins through Christ's death on the cross for me. I now invite Christ to again take His place on the throne of my life. Fill me with the Holy Spirit as You commanded me to be filled, and as You promised in Your Word that You would do if I asked in faith. I now thank You for directing my life and for filling me with the Holy Spirit."

Does this prayer express the desire of your heart? If so, ask God to fill you with the Holy Spirit right now and trust Him to do so.

How to know that you are filled (directed and empowered) with the Holy Spirit.

Did you ask God to fill you with the Holy Spirit? Do you know that you are now filled with the Holy Spirit? On what authority? (On the trustworthiness of God Himself and His Word: Hebrews 11:6; Romans 14:22, 23.)

Do not depend upon feelings. The promise of God's Word, not our feelings, is our authority. The Christian lives by faith (trust) in the trustworthiness of God Himself and His Word. This train diagram illustrates the relationship between fact (God and His Word), faith (our trust in God and His Word), and feeling (the result of our faith and obedience) (John 14:21).

The train will run with or without the caboose. However, it would be futile to attempt to pull the train by the caboose. In the same way, we, as Christians, do not depend upon feelings or emotions, but we place our faith (trust) in the trustworthiness of God and the promises of His Word.

How to walk in the Spirit

Faith (trust in God and in His promises) is the only means by which a Christian can live the Spirit-directed life. As you continue to trust Christ moment by moment:

1. Your life will demonstrate more and more of the fruit of the Spirit (Galatians 5:22, 23) and will be more and more conformed to the image of Christ (Romans 12:2; 2 Corinthians 3:18).
2. Your prayer life and study of God's Word will become more meaningful.
3. You will experience His power in witnessing (Acts 1:8).
4. You will be prepared for spiritual conflict against the world (1 John 2:15-17); against the flesh (Galatians 5:16-17); and against Satan (1 Peter 5:7-9; Ephesians 6:10-13).
5. You will experience His power to resist temptation and sin (1 Corinthians 10:13; Philippians 4:13; Ephesians 1:19-23; 2 Timothy 1:7; Romans 6:1-16).

Spiritual Breathing

By faith you can continue to experience God's love and forgiveness.

If you become aware of an area of your life (an attitude or an action) that is displeasing to the Lord, even though you are walking with Him and sincerely desiring to serve Him, simply thank God that He has forgiven your sins – past, present and future – on the basis of Christ's death on the cross. Claim His love and forgiveness by faith and continue to have fellowship with Him.

If you retake the throne of your life through sin – a definite act of disobedience – breathe spiritually.

Spiritual breathing (exhaling the impure and inhaling the pure) is an exercise in faith that enables you to continue to experience God's love and forgiveness.

1. **Exhale** – confess your sin – agree with God concerning your sin and thank Him for His forgiveness of it, according to 1 John 1:9 and Hebrews 10:1-25. Confession involves repentance - a change in attitude and action.
2. **Inhale** – surrender the control of your life to Christ, and appropriate (receive) the fullness of the Holy Spirit by faith. Trust that He now directs and empowers you; according to the command of Ephesians 5:18, and the promise of 1 John 5:14, 15.

Appendix 2
Merlin Carother's Experience of the Baptism

For some time I went to a small weekly prayer group near Fort Bragg. One evening, Ruth, a member of the group, was visibly moved during a prayer session. I had watched her during several meetings and often thought I would like to ask her how she had come to experience such obvious joy in her life. Unlike some of the rest of us, she seemed to be filled continuously with a joy I certainly had felt only on rare occasions in my life.

This particular evening Ruth confided in me: "I was so blessed I almost prayed out loud in tongues!" "You almost what?" I was horrified. "Prayed in tongues," Ruth said brightly. I lowered my voice and looked around to see if we were being watched. "Ruth, whatever has come over you?" Ruth laughed heartily. "I've been praying in tongues ever since I received the Baptism in the Holy Spirit." "What is that?" I'd never heard the term before. Ruth patiently explained that it was the same experience that the disciples had at Pentecost. "I experienced my own Pentecost." She smiled with unmistakable radiance. "I thought you were Baptist." I felt shaken. "I am, but God is moving in all denominations." I had heard rumors of a wave of emotionalism invading the churches. I had heard some tales about Pentecostals being "drunk in the spirit," whatever that meant, and having wild orgies. I knew Ruth needed help badly. I put my hand on her arm. "Be careful, Ruth," I said earnestly. "You're playing with dangerous stuff. I'll be praying for you, and if you need help, call me." Ruth smiled and patted my hand. "Thank you, Merlin. I appreciate your concern."

Some time later she called me. "Merlin, a group called Camp Farthest Out is having a retreat at Morehead City. We'd like you to go." It sounded like something I'd better stay away from. I tactfully replied that I would go if I could, which meant that I wouldn't be able to. Within the next week several others called. A businessman reminded me that I would need my golf clubs. A lady from Raleigh telephoned to tell me that she had arranged for all my expenses to be paid if I would go. Someone else called to say I could bring another minister free of charge. This was too much. How could I resist all this genuine interest in my spiritual well-being? I said, "Thank you, I'll go." I got in touch with a Presbyterian minister friend and invited him to come along. He hedged. "It's an all-expenses-paid trip at a resort hotel!" "I'll go." On the way Dick said: "Merlin, why are we going to this thing?" "I don't know," I said. "But it's free, so let's enjoy it."

In the hotel lobby we were greeted with such warm enthusiasm from people we'd never seen that I was beginning to wonder what kind of strange beings we had fallen amongst. The services were unlike anything we'd ever attended. People sang with uninhibited joy, clapped their hands, and actually raised their arms while they were singing. Both Dick and I felt very much out of place, but agreed there was a joy here from which we could learn something. One very cultured and refined-looking lady kept coming up to us and saying: "Has anything happened yet?" "No, ma'am, what do you mean?" we'd answer. "You'll see," she always said. Ruth and some of the others who had invited us urged me to have a private talk with a certain lady who they said had unusual power. They took us to meet her, and we sat patiently as she told us what God had done in her life and in the lives of others that she knew. She made numerous references to the "Baptism in the Holy Spirit," and went through the Scriptures to show that the experience had been a common one for Christians in the first century. "The Holy Spirit is still doing the same thing in many people's lives today," she said. "Jesus still baptizes those who believe in Him, just as He did at Pentecost."

I felt a twinge of excitement. Could it be that I could experience my own Pentecost? Could I see tongues of fire, hear the rush of wind, and speak in an unknown tongue? She had finished talking and sat looking at us. "I'd like to pray for you," she said softly. "That you might receive the Baptism in the Holy Spirit." Without hesitating I said, "Yes." She placed her hands on my head and began to pray softly. I waited for "it" to hit me. Nothing happened. I didn't feel a thing. She went on and placed her hands on Dick's head. When she had finished praying I looked at him and he looked at me. I could tell he hadn't felt anything either. This whole thing was a fake. The lady looked at us both with a hint of a smile. "You haven't felt anything yet, have you?" We shook our heads. "No, ma'am." "I'm going to pray for you in a language you will not understand. As I pray you will receive a new language of your own." Again she placed her hands on my head. I felt nothing, saw nothing, heard nothing. When she was through praying, she asked if I could hear or sense any words within me that I didn't understand. I thought for a minute and realized that there were in my mind words that didn't mean anything to me. I felt certain that these strange words were strictly a product of my own imagination, and I told her so. "If you said them out loud, would you feel as if you were being made a fool of?" she asked. "I certainly would." "Would you be willing to be a fool for Christ's sake?" This put the whole situation in a different perspective. Of course I'd do anything for Jesus, but speaking out loud such utter nonsense could mean disaster for my future. I could imagine all those people going around telling everyone that a Methodist chaplain had been praying in an unknown tongue. I might even have to leave the Army! Still, what if this was what Jesus wanted me to do? Suddenly even my Army career seemed less important.

Haltingly I began to speak out loud the words that were forming in my mind. Still I felt nothing different. I did believe that Jesus had given me a new tongue as a sign that He had baptized me in the Holy Spirit, yet the disciples at Pentecost had acted like drunk men. Obviously they had been overwhelmed by some feeling. I watched Dick; his experience seemed to be the same as mine. He spoke words of an unknown language and believed in the validity of it, yet displayed no emotional reaction. "Your experience is based on faith in a fact, not on feeling," said the lady, apparently reading our minds. I sat in deep thought. I didn't feel any different, but was I different? I looked up; an amazing realization had just hit me. "I once again know that Jesus Christ is alive!" I said. "I don't just believe, I KNOW!" Why, of course! The Holy Spirit brings witness of Jesus Christ, says the Bible. Now I knew that to be a fact. That was the source of the new authority of the disciples after Pentecost. They didn't remember a man who had lived and died and risen again. They knew Him in the present tense because He had filled them with His Holy Spirit, whose primary purpose is to witness about Jesus! Even as I saw the magnitude of my sin, I also saw Jesus in all His splendor as my redeemer. I saw Him for what I'd always known deep in my heart that He was. All of my recent nagging doubts were swept away by a wave of joyous certainty. It was glorious! Never again could I doubt that Jesus was who He said He was. Never again could I commit the folly of thinking that He had been a mere man, a good man, an example for us to follow. What a marvelous truth: Jesus living in us; His power operating through us. He is the vine. His life pulsates through our beings. We are nothing apart from Him, can do nothing in our own power. "Thank You, Jesus!"

I stood up, and as I reached my full height, something hit me! I was suddenly filled and overflowing with a feeling of warmth and love for everybody in the room. It must have hit Dick at the same time. I saw the tears well up in his eyes, and without a word we reached out and gave each other a bear hug, laughing and crying at the same time. We went downstairs for lunch, and I felt an overwhelming love for everyone I saw. I had never known anything like it. That evening Dick and I began to pray in one of the rooms. People came in to join us and soon the room was full. As we prayed, others were filled with the Holy Spirit. The hotel rang with shouts of joy as people experienced the fullness of Christ's presence. At 2:00 a.m. Dick and I tried to go to sleep. It was no use; we were too excited. I said: "Dick, let's get up and pray some more." We prayed another two hours for everyone we knew, and then praised God for His goodness to us.

Reprinted by permission of Foundation of Praise, California. Prison to Praise and other books by Merlin Carothers may be ordered at www.foundationofpraise.org.

www.ingramcontent.com/pod-product-compliance
Lightning Source LLC
Chambersburg PA
CBHW060312050426
42448CB00009B/1794